가장 최적의 시간이란 없다

죽기 전에 해야 할 77가지

이 책을 _____ 님께 바칩니다.

죽기 전에 해야 할 77가지

박홍이 지음 ∥ 함민우, 박홍이 그림

N 넥스웍

저자 박홍이

한때는 물리학과 낙제생이었으나 유학 후 물리학 박사가 되었다. 지금까지 국제 과학학술지 SCI에 반도체 실험과 관련한 논문 270편을 발표했는데 정년까지 300편을 채울 예정이라고 한다. 고등학교 시절 수영선수이기도 했던 그는 검도 5단에 공수도 4단의 유단자이다. 하루 3권의 책을 한꺼번에 읽는 독서광이며 수채화를 즐겨 그린다. 검도 복장을 한 모습이 멋있는, 깐깐하고 부드러운 물리학자이다.

죽기 전에 해야 할 77가지

초판 1쇄 발행	2011년 8월 15일
개정판 1쇄 발행	2014년 6월 2일
개정판 2쇄 발행	2018년 1월 19일

지은이	박홍이
그림	함민우, 박홍이
발행처	도서출판 넥스웍
발행인	최근봉

표지디자인	디자인길
편집디자인	김지은
주소	경기도 고양시 행신동 햇빛마을 2004동 1206호
전화	031)972-9207
팩스	031)972-9208
이메일	cntpchoi@naver.com
등록번호	제2014-000069호

이 도서의 저작권은 도서출판 넥스웍에 있으며
일부 혹은 전체내용을 무단 복사 전재하는 것은 저작권법에 저촉됩니다.
잘못된 책은 구입하신 서점에서 바꾸어 드립니다.

ISBN: 979-11-88389-03-2 (13320)

*값은 표지 뒷면에 표기되어 있습니다.

이 책이 모양을 갖추고 태어나도록
격려와 힘을 실어준 모든 분들이
함께 했기에 오늘의 기쁨을 함께 합니다.

서문

사람은 다 똑같이 태어나고, 또한 모두가 똑같은 죽음을 맞게 됩니다. 그러나 삶의 여정은 모두가 다르기에 세상에 슬픔도 힘든 일도 있습니다.

저의 짧은 인생 여정에서 오늘의 넘치는 축복의 삶은 제가 두 가지의 명제를 항상 가슴에 안고 살았기에 가능했습니다.

첫째는 절대로 마음먹은 일은 포기하지 않았고, 둘째는 꿈이 이루어지기까지 끝까지 최선을 다해서 노력했습니다.

26세의 나이에 미국으로 가서 대학교에 입학하여 고학으로 대학을 졸업하는 것으로 늦게 시작한 삶입니다만 오늘을 만드는 계기가 되었습니다.

아울러 마침내 18년 만에 자신과의 약속을 지켜 부산대학교에서 연세대 교수로 옮겨온 것도 포기하지 않고, 끈질기게 물고 늘어진 저의 고집스러움 때문입니다.

모두가 힘든 요즘, 모든 힘든 이에게 제가 이야기하고 싶은 것이 이 책의 내용입니다.

누구나 꿈을 가진 사람이라면 저와 같이 우직스럽게만 한다면, 그 꿈은 확실하게 이룬다는 확신을 전해드리고 싶었습니다.

힘든 시간은 지나가기 마련이지만, 강한 사람은 영원히 남는다는 사실을, 우리는 어제의 역사에서 많이 볼 수 있습니다. 포기하지 마시고, 이 험난한 상황에 굴복하지 마시고, 끝까지 꿈이 이루어질 때까지 최선을 다해서 삶의 전 과정에 많은 기쁨과 축복을 기도합니다.

차례

01 끝은 다시 시작임을 알아야 한다 15
    Learn to see the end of something as a new beginning.

02 성공하려면 늘 순간에 충실해라 17
    Know the value of every moment.

03 근원적으로 해결할 수 없는 문제는 그냥 껴안고 살아라 19
    Learn to live with a problem that has no solution.

04 모든 일에 완벽하기보다는 진일보함에 초점을 맞춰라 23
    Focus on progress rather than perfection.

05 최상의 시나리오를 생각하고 절망보나는 희망에 무게중심을 두어라 25
    Think the best-case scenario and dwell on the things that are uplifting.

06 모든 일에 감사하면 저절로 행복이 찾아온다 29
    Give thanks for everything for your happiness.

07 원하는 것만 말해라 31
    Speak only what you seek.

08 겁쟁이는 진짜 죽음을 맞기 전에 여러 번 죽는다 33
    The cowards die many times before their death.

09 모든 사람을 편견 없이 똑같이 대해라 35
    You treat everyone the same without a ny biased idea.

10 배움의 지름길은 연습과 코칭이다 37
    Practice and coaching are the two means
    by which we learn just about everything.

11 생각 자체가 내 모습이 된다 41
    You are what you think.

12 남이 나를 어떻게 보는지 신경 쓰기에 인생은 짧다 43
    Life is too short to worry about what others think.

13 모든 일을 흑백논리로 보지 말아라 47
Do not see thing in black and white.

14 지옥에 가서도 계속 하고 싶을 만큼 좋아할 수 있는 일을 찾아라 49
Discover something that you would die for.

15 긍정적으로 빨리 바뀌는 연습을 해라 51
Learn to be optimistic.

16 우리가 생각하는 가장 최적의 시간이란 없다 53
Do not wait for the right moment.

17 지금까지 넘어진 횟수보다 한 번만 더 일어나라 55
Get up just one more time than you fall.

18 가장 큰 수익을 얻으려면 자신에게 투자해라 59
Invest in yourself if you want a big return.

19 영원히 변하지 않는 법칙은 세상은 바뀐다는 것이다 61
The unchanged law of the universe is change.

20 세상에는 많은 종류의 사람이 있다 65
There are a lot of people in the world.

21 앞을 못 보는 사람이라면 개울을 원망하지 말아라 67
If you are blind, do not blame the ditch.

22 아무리 많은 구경을 해도 우리의 눈은 만족을 모른다 69
Our eyes can never see enough to be satisfied.

23 아무 문제없는 삶에서는 더 이상의 성장도 없다 73
Grow from your problem.

24 강을 건너야 할 사람에게 배가 되어 주어라 75
Become a boat for those rivers to cross.

25 현재에 살아라 79
Being in the present.

26 기회는 준비된 자에게만 주어진다 81
A chance is given to the prepared one.

27 빨리 우울함을 떨치는 법을 익혀라 85
    Learn to shake off blues of life.

28 적게 말하고 많이 행동해라 87
    Speak little, do much.

29 앉아야 할 때는 앉는 것에만 신경을 써라 89
    When you sit, just sit.

30 모든 일은 시작이 있으면 끝이 있다 93
    Everything that has a beginning has an ending.

31 내 운명을 스스로 창조해라 95
    Create your own destiny.

32 배수의 진을 쳐라 99
    Burn your bridge behind you.

33 둘이 하나보다 좋다 101
    Two is better than one.

34 두려움은 피하지 말고 직접 부딪혀라 105
    Beat fear through facing it.

35 가난은 내 마음의 상태이다 109
    Poor is your state of mind.

36 중요한 것은 어떻게든 시작하는 일이다 113
    The important thing is somehow to begin.

37 기회가 노크하지 않으면 노크할 수 있게 문을 만들어라 115
    Build a door if opportunity does not knock.

38 가는 길이 힘들다고 해서 길의 끝이 아니다 117
    A bend in the road is not the end of the road.

39 왜 살아야 하는지 이유가 있다 121
    Do have the reason to live for.

40 돈을 모은다는 것은 단지 결과물이다 125
    Wealth is a result.

41 완벽하기만을 바라지 마라 127
  We want to have our cake and eat it too.

42 실패는 돌아가는 길이다 131
  Think of failure as a detour.

43 삶을 100퍼센트 살아라 133
  Live life to its fullest.

44 가장 밝은 별은 가장 어두운 하늘에서 보인다 135
  The brightest star can be seen in the darkest sky.

45 상실은 가슴에 구멍이 나는 것과 같다 137
  Loss is a hole in our heart.

46 영원히 살 것처럼 배워라 141
  Learn as if you expected to live forever.

47 내면의 소리에 귀를 기울여라 143
  Listen to the inner voice of yours.

48 주어진 한계를 즐겨라 145
  Enjoy the limitation that is given to us.

49 아무도 듣지 않는다고 생각하고 노래해라 147
  Sing as if no one can hear you.

50 날마다 딱 한 번의 하루를 끝내라 151
  Finish each day and be done with it.

51 아픔을 선생님으로 대접해라 153
  Treat pain as a teacher.

52 첫걸음이 가장 힘든 법이다 155
  The first step is the hardest.

53 삶의 전 과정을 철저히 즐겨라 157
  Enjoy the process of life.

54 사랑에서 평화와 행복을 마음껏 누려라 159
  Find peace and happiness in love.

55 자신을 믿으면 더 잘할 수 있다 163
We can do well if we believe ourselves.

56 어둠을 벗어나려면 촛불을 켜라 165
Light a candle if we want to eliminate darkness.

57 사막을 만나면 정원으로 만들어라 167
When we meet a desert, make it a garden.

58 남이 갈 수 없는 곳으로 가야 성공할 수 있다 171
To go where other people could not go.

59 새로운 도전을 감사하게 받아라 173
The challenge will not wait.

60 가능한 한 많이 비워두어라 175
Let us remain as empty as possible.

61 우리는 무한한 가능성을 가진 한 사람의 신이다 177
You are one of the Lords of the earth with unlimited potentials.

62 사실들이 꿈보다 더 중요하다 179
Facts are better than dreams.

63 분명한 목표가 있기에 운명은 만들어간다 181
Purpose shapes destiny.

64 단 일 초의 시간도 낭비하지 말고 늘 깨어서 투자해라 183
Do not waste and be willing to invest.

65 행운이란 시작에 불과하다 185
Luck is only a beginning.

66 평소 적게 베풀면 어려울 때 똑같은 대접을 받는다 187
If you give little, you will get little.

67 겉으로 드러나는 현상만 보고 판단하지 말아라 189
Do not judge anything by appearance.

68 일인자가 되려면 많은 시간과 노력을 쏟아라 191
Be the master in whatever you undertake.

69 남들과 똑같이 생각해서는 새로운 창조란 없다 195
    Do not think like the crowd.

70 자유의지대로 가난해져라 197
    Choose poverty with poverty own free will.

71 절실히 원하는 대로 말하고 행동해라 199
    Yon can remake yourself if you want to.

72 갈림길에서 헤맬 때는 가슴이 원하는 길로 가라 201
    When you come to a fork the road, follow the voice of your heart.

73 행동은 내가 선택한 것이다 203
    Your action is your choice.

74 경청을 한다는 것은 사랑의 표현이다 205
    Listening is an act of love.

75 어떠한 일도 그 일에 맞는 적절한 시간을 기다려라 207
    We need the power of waiting for the right moment.

76 결승점에 가까이 왔다 해도 천천히 달리면 안 된다 209
    You do not need to slow down when you see the finishing line in a race.

77 흐르는 물결을 따라서 흐르는 강과 하나가 되어라 211
    Swim with the current and become one with river.

There are many things we have to learn in a journey called life. When we face the last moment of our day on earth, we might have many things to go over and try to convey our thoughts on life to our beloved ones. A coin has two sides and so do our lives - life and death. Life gives us good and bad things alike. All we have to do is to tackle everything that comes along. Especially we have to take a stand in time of hardship. The saying goes, 'When one door closes, another door opens.' It will give us promising up words for our down days. Different attitudes alone can produce completely different results and always we have to remain positive. We must learn to turn lemons into lemonade in such a way that we can see the light at the end of tunnel called hard times. Just keep in mind we have everything in us that we need to succeed. Life is often like a play we adopt roles based on our mental images. Remain positive on all occasions and be the winner in life.

The Last Letters 5 minutes permitting

01
끝은 다시 시작임을 알아야 한다

Learn to see the end of something
as a new beginning.

만약 생의 마지막 순간을 맞이하게 되면, 당신은 평소 사랑했던 사람들에게 무슨 말을 남기겠습니까? 동전이 앞뒷면이 있듯이, 인생에는 삶과 죽음이 있고, 좋은 일도 나쁜 일도 똑같이 일어납니다. 일이 오면 일을 처리하고, 특히 힘든 일이 있을 때에는 버겁지만 감당해내야 하는 것이 우리의 숙명입니다. 이런 격언이 있습니다. '한 개의 문이 닫히면, 다른 또 하나의 문이 열린다.' 분명 일을 대하는 태도에 따라 결과도 다르게 나타나는 법입니다. 삶이 우리에게 나쁜 것을 주면, 그 나쁜 것을 좋은 것으로 만드는 재주를 부려 봅시다. 힘든 시기에는 더욱 더 희망을 볼 수 있어야 합니다. 내 안에는 성공에 필요한 모든 것이 있음을 반드시 기억합시다. 항상 긍정적으로 남읍시다. 삶은 마치 연극과 같아서 우리가 머릿속에 그리는 상태로 적응하게 되어 있습니다. 그러므로 모든 일에 긍정적으로 생각하고 삶에서 성자로 자리매김하는 것이 어떤지요?

A right time for everything exists in our days on earth. This time may be termed as the moment that we meet in our lives. A moment will build the life span of our lives and our lives will be evaluated through how we spent every moment of our lives. Also we grow up in a sea of moment. 'Winners will know the value of every moment and do spend the moment with their best efforts.' Sometimes just relaxing will be the very best thing one can do at the moment and another time it requires one does act like spending the last moment of one's life.

There are many ways to reach the peak of a mountain and we also keep it mind that the variety is the spice of life. We are more apt at not seeing the forest for the tree in life due to our ignorance on wisdom of life. Wisdom of life can be gained through reading books, meeting people of all walks of life, and thinking much on what one had learned on oner's everyday life. Another alternative way can be as: Read much, think much, and write much. We are born to win in a game called life and the official guide to success is to know the value of every moment and utilizing it to the full extent of one's power.

The Last Letters 5 minutes permitting

02
성공하려면
늘 순간에 충실해라

Know the value of every moment.

인생에서 일어나는 모든 일들은 항상 합당한 시간에 일어납니다. 이 시간을 '순간'이라고 정의할 수 있습니다. 순간들이 쌓여서 생애를 이루고, 나중에 살아온 나의 생애에 대해 사람들의 평가를 받게 됩니다. 다시 말하지만, 우리는 수많은 순간순간을 겪으며 성장합니다. '승리하는 사람은 모든 순간의 가치를 알고 그 순간에 적합한 일을 하는 사람입니다.' 쉬는 것이 최선일 때도 있고, 삶의 마지막을 맞이하듯 보내는 것이 최선일 때도 있지요.

산의 정상에 도달하는 길은 한 가지만 있는 것이 아닙니다. 다양성이란 삶을 멋지게 만드는 향신료와도 같으므로, 항상 여러 방향으로 생각하는 습관을 가지십시오. 하지만 우리는 무지해서 나무는 보고 숲을 못 보는 오류를 빈번히 저지릅니다. 삶의 지혜는 어떻게 얻어질까요? 많이 읽고, 많이 생각하고, 많이 글을 쓰면 자연스레 터득된다고 말할 수 있습니다. 성공하고 싶은가요? 그렇다면 지금 이 순간에 최선을 다하십시오.

In lifers journey we meet many obstacles that we have to overcome. There are things about which we can not do anything within our ability. There is a saying that goes. "What can not be cured must be endured." We are designed such that if we can not stand a certain limit of our strength, we are going to be broken down. Just imagine you are facing your death, you had better accept your death with grace rather than struggle with it. Terminal cancer patients are supposed to learn to accept their death with grace such that they can expect the wonder of their after life rather than the pain of their death. Life has the symmetry such that one can see the bright side along with dark side. Thus we have to try harder to see the sunny side of our lives. When one is at the final moment of their life, do expect the coming new life that one is going to face. The death will come and there is no way of preventing it within our ability. Do learn to accept the inevitability and face the inevitability with grace given to us with the grace of God. 'When we pass away, we are going to turn into dust that is the origin of our lives. Learn the inevitability with loving-kindness for your days to come.'

The Last Letters 5 minutes permitting

03
근원적으로 해결할 수 없는 문제는 그냥 껴안고 살아라

Learn to live with a problem that has no solution.

우리 앞에는 넘어야 할 많은 문제들이 있습니다. 그중에는 우리 능력으로 도저히 해결 불가능한 문제도 있습니다. "고칠 수 없는 병은 참아야 한다."는 말도 있지요. 우리는 자신의 한계를 넘어서면 몸이 부서지게 되어 있습니다. 가령 죽음을 마주한다고 합시다. 그때는 죽음과 싸우기보다는 우아하게 죽음을 받아들이는 것이 더 좋습니다. 마지막 고비에 온 암 환자는 죽음의 고통을 생각하기보다는 새로운 세상을 경이의 마음으로 받아들이는 것이 더 나은 선택입니다. 잊지 마십시오. 삶은 대칭으로 존재하기에 좋은 면도 있고 나쁜 면도 있다는 것을! '죽으면 먼지로 변해서 다시 태어난 곳으로 간다는 사실을 되새겨야 합니다. 피할 수 없는 문제에 맞닥뜨리면 우아하게 인애(仁愛)로써 받아들이고 내일을 맞이하십시다.'

"Over the mountains, there are mountains."

산 넘어 산이다.

- Korean proverb -

On the road of our lives we often seek perfection on everything and more often than not we are dissatisfied with what we got. It is better seeking progress rather than perfection on every task we are involved in. We are not made perfect like God in doing things. God is perfect and we are willing to imitate God during our lives. 'Just be satisfied on the little progress you made today over yesterday's and learn to enjoy your numbered days on earth.' Everything gives us different meanings depending on how we think. Learn to think differently and rise above the world's standard. God loves us and gives us all we need to be the winner in life. Our mental attitudes will do us miracles over miracles as long as we retain positive rather than negative mental frames. All changes are made through thinking. Let's think differently and get what we want to have for our joy-filled days. God is real and He wants you to be happy and enjoy joy-filled life of your own. Also in doing a new project aims on the progress rather than perfection.

The Last Letters 5 minutes permitting

04
모든 일에 완벽하기보다는 진일보함에 초점을 맞춰라

Focus on progress rather than perfection.

우리는 모든 일에 완벽함을 추구합니다. 혹여 일이 잘못되면 욕구 불만이 쌓입니다. 자, 이제부터 우리가 하는 일에 완벽함보다는 진일보함에 초점을 맞춥시다. 신은 완벽하지만 우리는 그렇지 못함을 인정하기만 하면 됩니다. '어제보다 오늘 진일보함에 만족하고 남은 생을 즐기십시오.' 모든 일은 생각의 산물입니다. 다르게 생각할 줄 알고 세상의 잣대를 넘어설 줄 알아야 합니다. 생각을 긍정적으로 가지면 기적이 함께 할 수 있고, 생각을 달리하면 기쁨이 넘치는 날들로 가득해집니다.

During our lives we face with many circumstances and many problems that have to be solved. Do think the best-case scenario rather than the worst-case one. There are always two choices in viewing a case, positive or negative views. Do dwell on the positive so that we can have the bright days to come. God wants us to be happy and lead a joy-filled life. We have everything to lead a successful life and this life can be achieved through changing the frame of our mind. Guard our heart above all else, for it determines the course of our lives. We are what we think and our belief will make us what we want to be. That's why we have to dwell on the positive side rather than negative side. If we think we can, we can and that's what we have to inscribe on our heart for more bountiful and blessed days of our lives. 'Think of the sunny day even if all we can see is the cloud above our head.' Do expect the best even if we are facing the worst-case situation right now. God will do us a miracle if we stick to the last just believing the belief that we will win to the end with the help of our almighty God.

The Last Letters 5 minutes permitting

05
최상의 시나리오를 생각하고 절망보다는 희망에 무게중심을 두어라

Think the best-case scenario and
dwell on the things that are uplifting.

삶이란 늘 풀어야 할 숙제들로 가득 차 있습니다. 그 숙제를 풀려면 중요한 핵심만 알면 됩니다. 핵심은 늘 좋은 시나리오에 초점을 맞추는 것입니다. 우리에게 일어나는 일마다 긍정적으로도 혹은 부정적으로도 볼 수 있습니다만, 항상 긍정적으로 보는 사람에게 내일의 밝은 날이 있는 법입니다. 하나님은 우리의 삶이 행복하고 기쁨에 젖어 살기를 원하십니다. 우리는 성공에 필요한 모든 능력을 갖추었지만 제대로 발휘하지 못합니다. 왜 그럴까요? 당신의 가슴을 활짝 열어젖혀야 합니다. 할 수 있다는 생각으로 가슴을 채워야 합니다. '머리 위에 온통 구름만 있다 해도, 구름 위에는 반드시 감추어진 햇빛이 있다는 믿음을 가지십시오. 이 믿음이 우리를 최후의 승리지로 만들어갈 것입니다.'

The happiness of Diogenes can be found under the bright sun.
The sunshine gives happiness to Diogenes.
Alexander the Great found his happiness
through conquering many countries.
They have different ways of being happy.

Put it in a nutshell
building up inward power of the soul
is the way to happiness.

찬사
Praise

행복이란?
Happiness?

디오게네스의 행복은
따뜻한 햇볕을 쬐는 것이었다고 한다.
알렉산더 대왕의 행복은 많은 나라를 점령하는 것이었다.
각각의 잣대로 둘 다 각자의 행복을 즐겼을 것이다.

궁극적으로 보자면,
내적인 영혼의 힘을 키우는 것이
행복한 삶에 이르는 최선의 방법이다.

출처: 만화 30원(야스미디어)

돈
Money

건배
Cheer-up

명예
Glory

God wants you to be happy and the first thing to do for your happiness is to give thanks for everything. Your life is like a flowing river and the life of the river is just like your life. The river runs its allotted distance until it reaches the sea. Sometimes it runs slow and sometimes it runs fast. The river does show us turbulent flow along with calm flow like your days on earth. The ups and downs are what you face everyday in your life. Do learn to give the prayer of thanksgiving in down days for the coming up days so you can see the sun at the end of cloudy days. Life is an ongoing process and you will meet varieties of events during your lifetime. When you stumble over difficulties of life, do remember that the tough times never last but tough people do last. Learning to give the prayer of thanksgiving on rough going is the first step toward happy life.

'If you can give thanks on rough going, your days will be brighter than before and the good tidings of life will be given to you without stop.' Life can be compared to a flowing river and you just enjoy the every moment of your days like a flowing river that enjoys its journey toward the sea.

The Last Letters 5 minutes permitting

06
모든 일에 감사하면
저절로 행복이 찾아온다

Give thanks for everything for your happiness.

당신의 행복을 위해 모든 일에 감사하십시오. 삶은 흐르는 강물과 같습니다. 강물은 그저 자기에게 주어진 길을 따라서 바다까지 흘러갑니다. 가끔은 천천히, 가끔은 빠르게……. 조용히 흐르다가도 가끔은 소용돌이도 치면서……. 우리의 삶도 마찬가지입니다. 일이 잘되다가도 내리막길을 내달리기도 합니다. 마치 흐르는 강처럼, 여러 가지 일들을 겪습니다. 힘든 일과 부닥치더라도 시간이 지나면 언제 그랬냐는 듯 지나가기 마련입니다. 진짜 강한 사람은 어려운 일도 시간과 함께 결국 극복된다는 단순함을 알지요. 오히려 이 난관이 행복으로 가기 위한 시작임을 알고 감사기도를 올립니다.

'상황이 좋은 때가 아니라 극심히 힘든 때 감사기도를 할 수 있다면, 큰 복이 기다릴 것입니다.' 삶은 흐르는 강과 같아서, 강물이 바다로 갈 때까지 모든 순간을 하나도 빼지 않고 즐기듯이 우리도 매 순간을 즐기십시다.

The action creates the feeling and the feeling leads you toward the goal that you want to achieve in your life. What and how you speak in everyday life are the most important matter in your life. 'What you speak creates the image and the image stored in your subconscious mind will create your days to come.' If you want to amass a fortune in future, you just talk or speak about money and think about how to make it in such a way that your subconscious mind will do the job. If you want to be a millionaire, you do act like a millionaire. Your action creates the millionairess mind and you are on the road to become a millionaire. Nothing comes free in life and there is a saying that goes, "No pain. No gain." Think twice before you speak so that what you speak will activate to achieve your goal in life. If you want your kids to become dream kids whom you have in mind, you should speak or talk to your kids what you wished in your heart. Speak only what you seek.

The Last Letters 5 minutes permitting

07
원하는 것만 말해라

Speak only what you seek.

날마다 나는 어떤 말을 하며, 어떻게 말하느냐가 나의 삶을 결정하는 중요한 요인이 될 수 있습니다. '입에서 나오는 말은 하나의 이미지를 만듭니다. 그리고 그 이미지가 잠재의식에 저장되어 미래를 만들어 가기 때문입니다.' 백만장자가 되려면 항상 돈에 대해서 이야기하고, 어떻게 돈을 만들 것인가를 심각하게 고민해야 합니다. 말하고 고민하는 가운데 잠재의식에 쌓여 백만장자의 감정이 피 속에 흐르게 되고, 당신은 어느 순간 백만장자가 돼 있을 것입니다. 아이들이 당신이 원하는 모습으로 성장하길 바란다면, 아이들에게 그 모습 그대로 말하고 행동으로 보여주면 됩니다. 세상에는 공짜가 없기에 힘든 과정이 필요한 법입니다. 이제부터라도 무슨 말을 하기 전에 한 번 더 생각하고 말하는 습관을 가집시다.

In reality of life you face the death just once but you may face many deaths according to your deeds in your life. Try to lead your life such that you face your death only once. The braves will meet their death just once through acting like the valiant. When you deal with the matters of life like the cowards do, you will experience many deaths. Do live your days like the valiant do and you will meet your final day with grace in your heart. 'God wants you to be brave enough to deal with everything with grace since you are endowed with God's grace from birth.' You are what you think and do act like the valiant in all circumstances in your days on earth. Do remind you of that you are going to face death just once in your life like the valiant.

The Last Letters 5 minutes permitting

08
겁쟁이는 진짜 죽음을 맞기 전에 여러 번 죽는다

The cowards die many times before their death.

죽음은 일생에 딱 한 번만 겪습니다. 하지만 겁쟁이는 대개 여러 번 죽음을 맛봅니다. 가능하면 한 번의 죽음만 맞이하도록 힘쓰십시오. 용감한 사람은 용감한 사람답게 죽음을 한 번만 맞습니다. 삶의 문제를 겁쟁이마냥 두려움에 떨며 행하면 여러 번 죽을 수밖에 없습니다. 하나님은 우리가 모든 일에 우아하게 의연함으로 대처하기를 원하십니다. 용감하게 말입니다. '모든 일은 마음먹은 대로 되는 것이기에 용감하게 마음먹고 의연하게 행동합시다.' 용감한 사람처럼 죽음을 한 번만 맞이합시다.

God treats everyone the same. God never shows more favor toward the rich or the learned since God sees what one has in one's heart. You do learn God's way of treating people so that you never fall short in judging people through their outward appearance. A tree is judged by the fruits it bears and so should you judge others through their conduct. People speak what they keep in their heart. We are brothers and sisters in the eyes of our Lord so treat others with brotherly love and kindness without any biased idea. 'If you want to be treated right by our Lord, you have to treat your neighbors with the same rules that God judges us.' You should watch your judging heart with more strict rules such that you are not being judged by our Lord in your final day with the same rules. Sometimes we miss the forest for the tree due to our biased idea on all things. Try harder to learn the wisdom of our Lord on all things during your life. God treats everyone the same.

The Last Letters 5 minutes permitting

09
모든 사람을 편견 없이 똑같이 대해라

You treat everyone the same without any biased idea.

하나님은 모든 사람을 똑같이 대하십니다. 가진 자나 더 많이 배운 사람이라고 특별하게 대하시지 않습니다. 하나님은 대신 그 사람의 마음속에 담긴 생각을 보십니다. 나무는 과실로 판단되듯이, 사람은 그 사람의 행동으로 판단되어야 옳습니다. '하나님께서 우리를 공평하게 판단하시기를 원한다면, 우리도 이웃을 바르게 판단해야 옳겠지요.' 반대로 하나님께서 왜곡하여 판단하시기를 원치 않는다면 나 역시 이웃을 왜곡하여 판단해서도 안 됩니다. 편견으로 인해 나무는 보고 숲을 보지 못하는 우매한 판단을 하지 말아야 합니다. 하나님의 지혜를 배우십시오. 하나님은 모두를 똑같이 대하십니다.

We learn our way of living through experience of our own and experience of others. There is a saying and it goes, "Experience keeps a dear school." This saying tells us the value of experience on all matters in life. Life wants us to go through many roads of life to appreciate the value of our lives on earth, but our days are numbered to cover the entire spectrum of life. The vicarious observation and experience of others will give us the required experience of the less traveled roads of our lives's experience. This will be found in books. Books are born through endeavors of human beings and books mold the ways of life for human beings. We can not overemphasize the value of reading and the importance of reading. We have to read extensively on all matters of life to be taught how to lead our lives. For example, lessons from the lives of famous people can be found on books. Read voraciously such that you can say a thing about all matters of life. 'Leaders are readers in the history of human being and be a leader in your field of specialization through reading much.'

The Last Letters 5 minutes permitting

10
배움의 지름길은 연습과 코칭이다

Practice and coaching are the two means
by which we learn just about everything.

"경험이 가장 비싼 학교다."라는 속담이 있습니다. 경험은 인생을 빨리 터득하는 지름길이지만, 우리의 살아갈 날은 한정되어 있고 경험도 매우 제한적일 수밖에 없지요. 그러므로 간접경험이라도 많이 해봐야 하는데 이를 위해서 사실 책만한 것이 없습니다. 책은 여러 사람의 경험으로 이루어지고, 다양한 갈래의 인생을 간접적으로라도 맛볼 수 있습니다. 책읽기는 아무리 강조해도 모자랍니다. 가령 성공을 이룬 위대한 사람들이 겪었던 인생의 교훈을 책은 단번에 알려주니 공짜로 인생을 배우는 게 아닌가요? 세상의 모든 위대한 지도자들은 한결같이 책을 많이 읽었다고 합니다. '지금 힘쓰는 분야에서 최고의 지도자로 자리 매김하려면 책을 가까이 두어야 합니다.'

"Blur the line between work and play."

일과 놀이의 구분을 하지 말아야 한다.

- Arther Toynbee -

If you think the positive side of a matter, you are going to get the positive result according to your faith. Like attracts like and the positive attracts positive results. Just imagine you feed your brain with negative thoughts. What do you expect to get from your brain as outputs? Definitely you are going to get negative outputs since you have planted and nourished your brain with the seed of negative thoughts. If you want the positive results in all matters in life, do think positively for your own good. The power of positive thinking gives you the unlimited power to achieve your goal and you have to keep this idea in your heart all through your life. 'It is your frame of mind to determine the outputs of your endeavors in everything you do in your life.' Try to think positive and get the positive results in everything you do. There is a saying, "Junk in and junk out." Empty your heart of all negative thoughts and fill it with all positive thoughts for your bright days to come.

The Last Letters 5 minutes permitting

11
생각 자체가
내 모습이 된다

You are what you think.

문제의 긍정적인 면을 지속적으로 생각하면, 그 생각이 가져온 믿음으로 마침내 긍정적인 결과를 얻을 수 있습니다. 만약 뇌에 부정적인 생각을 계속해서 주입하면 어떠한 결과를 얻게 될까요? 당연히 부정적인 생각이 부정적인 결과를 가져오게 됩니다. 그러므로 만약 긍정적인 결과를 얻길 원한다면 긍정적으로 생각하면 됩니다. 긍정의 힘은 무한합니다. 가슴에 담은 목표가 있다면 꼭 이룰 수 있다고 긍정합시다. "나는 꼭 그렇게 되고 말 거야." '생각의 틀이 삶의 모든 것을 결정한다는 것을 알고 긍정적으로 생각하십시오.' 이런 속담이 있습니다. "쓰레기를 넣으면 쓰레기가 나온다."

Many people led their lives according to the standards of others and ended their lives terribly. Your life is all yours to plan and enjoy to the fullest. On your deathbed what you want to say to your beloved on your life. As long as your life does not disturb the peace of your neighbors or your community, you can lead your life as you wished. Life is too short to worry away or live to the expectation of others. You are the architect of your life and do plan your life in advance preparing for the days to come. There are things to consider in preparing your coming days. If you are too eager to amass wealth, your life will go astray in coming days. Wealth is a result of your endeavors and you are supposed to do the required job with all your might. As you sow so you reap. This simple adage is all you have to keep in your heart. Be a boss rather than a servant in leading your life so that you might be happy on your deathbed. 'The surest way to be happy on your last day is leading your life according to your way.'

The Last Letters 5 minutes permitting

12
남이 나를 어떻게 보는지 신경 쓰기에 인생은 짧다

Life is too short to worry about what others think.

많은 사람들이 타인의 기준에 따라 자신의 삶을 살아가기에 소중한 삶을 형편없이 살아갑니다. 인생을 충분히 계획하고 즐기는 것은 우리에게 주어진 몫입니다. 죽음을 맞이하면서 사랑하는 사람에게 살아온 인생에 대해 무슨 이야기를 해주려고 합니까? 남에게 피해를 주지 않는 선에서 우리가 원하는 방향으로 마음껏 살아봅시다. 남의 시선 걱정하고 남의 기대에 맞추어 살기에 인생은 너무나 짧습니다. 인생이라는 집을 내가 건축가가 되어 설계하고 계획한 대로 착실하게 진행하십시오. 행복한 죽음을 맞기 위해 내 인생을 종이 아닌 주인으로 당당히 살아갑시다. '행복에 다다르는 가장 확실한 길은 나의 삶을 나의 뜻대로 사는 것입니다.'

Things that you piled up all through your life
without thinking.
The shrouds have no pockets.

분만실-출생
Maternity ward-Born

생존경쟁의 장-생존
Survival Training Center-Survival

지상에서의 네 가지 과정
Four phases on earth.

디오게네스의 행복은
허겁지겁 쌓아올린 물욕들.
그러나 수의에는 주머니가 없다.

출처 : 만화 30원(야스미디어)

응급실-병듦
Emergency Room-Sick

장례식장-죽음
Funerdl Home-Death

It is easy to see things in black and white and we do many judgments through this frame of mind. We may make many mistakes through a simpleminded approach in judging things and people around us. If you do not want to be judged by others, you should not judge others with black and white frame of judging standard. There is a gray along with many different colors in nature like many different frames of standard to see things through. Do try to get the holistic view on all matters rather than Cartesian view which emphasizes dichotomy in all things. There are many sides in all matters and it is a wise way to see things through many points of view. Life shows us many panoramic views on all matters and it is wise to learn many views on all matters too. No one looks alike, no land is alike, and so is one's view on life. 'Do remind you of ever-changing views on all matters and do not see things in black and white since nothing stays permanent.'

The Last Letters 5 minutes permitting

13
모든 일을 흑백논리로 보지 말아라

Do not see thing in black and white.

모든 일을 판단할 때 흑 아니면 백으로 보는 것이 사실 가장 쉽습니다. 하지만 단순명쾌한 듯 보이는 이 흑백논리는 실수를 저지르기 쉬운 지름길입니다. 검정색과 흰색만 있는 것이 아니라 회색도 있고 여러 종류의 색깔을 통해서 판단할 잣대가 있습니다. 만약 남이 나를 흑백논리로 판단한다면 기분이 좋지 않겠지요. 모든 일에는 한 가지로만 설명할 수 없는 다양한 면이 있기에 총체적으로 보는 방식이 데카르트식의 이분법으로 보는 방식보다 훨씬 현명한 방법입니다. 사람마다 생긴 모습이 다르고 각자 인생을 바라보는 견해도 다릅니다. 또한 '이 세상의 모든 일이란 계속 변합니다. 흑백논리로 설명하기엔 이 세상은 변화무쌍하다는 말씀입니다.'

Doing things that you love to do is the basic idea in choosing your career in life. How do you know the career you have to choose for living? There should be many trials and errors before you find the career you love to do. In order to be an expert in any field, one has to do many failed attempts so that one can find the career that one has to do for life. If you want to find something that you would die for, you should not be afraid of failure on what you have tried. Practice makes perfect even on failure that you face everyday. Failure teaches us how we circumvent the failure in future. Life itself is an ongoing process and you never ever give up on finding something that you would die for. Even if you are facing the last moment of your life, you never stop finding the career for your new life in the world to come after you pass away. 'Working that you love to do will put you in paradise even if you are in hell.'

The Last Letters 5 minutes permitting

14
지옥에 가서도 계속 하고 싶을 만큼 좋아할 수 있는 일을 찾아라

Discover something that you would die for.

자신이 가장 좋아하는 일을 직업으로 선택하십시오. 어떻게 가장 좋아하는 일을 찾을 수 있을까요? 우선 실패를 두려워하지 말아야 합니다. 날마다 실패하더라도 연습이 완벽함에 이르게 하고, 내일은 실패를 비껴가는 법을 알려줍니다. 삶은 계속되는 과정이므로, 목숨 걸 만한 일을 발견할 때까지 절대로 포기하지 말아야 합니다. 죽음을 맞는 순간까지도 포기하지 말아야 합니다. 그리고 죽어서도 마찬가지입니다. '만약 지옥에 가서도 이 일이 너무 좋아 계속할 수 있다면 이 일이 당신을 천당으로 보내줄 것입니다.'

A few years ago a friend of mine was diagnosed as a malignant pancreatic cancer and the doctor told him of his final day on earth. My friend was so depressed and left a journey of his choosing. He went to India and worked for the poor and needy people in India, especially the untouchable. The miracle happened to my friend and he has lived to this day without any ailment. Just by not attaching to his life, he has won the grace of our Lord. When you are attached to something, you are going to screw up the thing you attach to. By detachment you will get the thing that you cherish in your life. Life shows us the way in which we can obtain things we want by changing our mental attitude toward things. Being positive means we have to learn the way of detaching things that are precious to us like our lives. Also being positive means to accept things as they come even if it means our death. God wants us to be the winner in life on all things and we have to be optimistic on all matters and in all circumstances. 'By clinging to life, we are losing our lives whereas by detachment we can have the everlasting lives of our own. Always try to see the bright side of a thing rather than the dark for your sunny days to come.'

The Last Letters 5 minutes permitting

15
긍정적으로 빨리 바뀌는 연습을 해라

Learn to be optimistic.

얼마 전 친구 한 명이 병원에서 곧 암으로 죽는다는 사실을 선고받았습니다. 이 친구는 너무 실망이 되어 곧바로 여행을 떠나버리더군요. 그리고 인도에 가서 가난하고, 도움을 필요로 하는 사람들, 특히 불가촉천민을 위해서 일했습니다. 그런데 이 친구에게 놀라운 기적이 일어났습니다. 그는 의사가 선고한 시간이 한참 지났는데도 현재까지 말짱히 살아 있습니다. 스스로 병이라는 굴레에서 벗어나자 하나님의 은총을 받은 것입니다. 어떤 일에 집착하면 스스로의 집착으로 인해 모든 일을 망칩니다. 마음을 비우기만 하면 필요한 모든 것을 얻을 수 있습니다! 간단하지요? 긍정이란 달리 말하면 어떤 대단한 것에도 집착을 버리는 겁니다. 설사 죽음의 순간이 오더라도 하나님은 우리가 의연하게 죽음을 긍정하길 원하십니다. '아이러니하게도 생명에 집착하면 생명을 잃게 되고, 집착하지 않으면 영생을 얻을 수 있습니다.'

The right moment is within your reach whenever you try to do a new thing in your life but the right moment of your choosing may be different from the right moment of the thing you try. The unseen almighty knows the right moment of all things and will bestow you the thing you want in the right moment. All we have to do is doing our very best efforts all the time of our lives. If you wait the right moment of a thing to achieve your goal in life, you will never achieve anything in your life because you will idle away your life just waiting. Do what you can at every moment of your life and God will give the right moment along with all the good things to achieve your goal in life. We should live our lives rather than existing as an animal called human being. Life has to create something out of nothing such that life gives meaning on existence. Do struggle rather than idle away your time on all occasions. 'The right moment will be given to you through many trials of your undefeated attempts on all matters. God helps those who help themselves.'

The Last Letters 5 minutes permitting

16
우리가 생각하는 가장 최적의 시간이란 없다

Do not wait for the right moment.

어떤 일을 수행할 때 가장 수월한 최적의 시간이란 것이 있는 법인데, 우리가 생각하는 시간과 사뭇 다를 수 있습니다. 보이지 않는 하나님께서는 이 최적의 시간을 아시고 자연스레 알맞은 시간에 원하는 일을 할 수 있도록 허락하십니다. 사실 우리가 할 일은 그저 그 주어진 시간 동안에 최선을 다하는 것뿐입니다. 우리가 스스로 최적의 시간을 마냥 기다린다면 결국 허송세월을 보내게 됩니다. 현재 감당해야 할 일에 머뭇거리지 말고 정진합시다. 인간인 우리는 인간다운 삶을 살아야지 동물처럼 생존하는 것만으로는 안 됩니다. '매사에 열심히 투쟁하듯이 살고 절대로 적당히 살지 맙시다. 하늘은 스스로 돕는 자를 돕습니다.'

In lifers journey we meet many difficulties along with having many defeats on our attempted adventures on life. Every time you fall, just get up and do try without stopping till you succeed. Life is an ongoing process and all we have to do is keeping on trying on what we do. Our going has to go even if it does not go with our liking. We have a bright sun one day and we have a rainy day in other times like our lives in general. 'Life shows us the inherent symmetry on all matters like a valley can not exist without peaks, a river without its banks. Thus ups and downs are the existing symmetry of our lives.' Do act more bravely with a big dream in your heart on all matters of life so that you will stand head up in all circumstances of life. If you have sunny days all the year round, you might have drought and this might be more serious problem than sunny days.

The balancing in life is important and this can be learned through defeats. Try to get up one more time than you fall for your better life.

The Last Letters 5 minutes permitting

17
지금까지 넘어진 횟수보다 한 번만 더 일어나라
Get up just one more time than you fall.

삶은 좋으나 싫으나 계속 살아가는 일입니다. 지금 하는 일이 내 뜻처럼 흘러가지 않을 때도 그 일을 계속해야만 합니다. 살다 보면 햇빛이 날 때도 있고 비가 오는 날도 있습니다. '삶 속에는 내재하는 대칭이 존재합니다. 마치 산꼭대기는 골짜기가 없이는 존재하지 못하고, 강은 강둑이 없으면 존재할 수 없듯이. 잘되고 못되는 것이 삶에 내재하는 대칭입니다.' 큰 꿈으로 대담하게 모든 일을 대하면, 아무리 어려운 일도 의연히 대처할 수 있습니다. 만약 일 년 사시사철 햇빛만 있다면 어떨까요? 가뭄으로 더 큰 피해를 보겠지요. 그래서 삶에서 균형이 중요한 것입니다. 그리고 이 균형은 실패에서 배우게 됩니다. 그러니 넘어지면 꼭 한 번만 더 일어나십시오.

"If you bite your lip and understand that this is the only world, you will endure."

입술을 깨물고 지금 가진 세상이
세상의 끝인 것을 알면 참을 수 있다.

- <Native Speaker>, by Changrae Lee -

A thousand mile journey starts with one step you initiated at the beginning of your journey. Rome was not built in a day and so are our goals in life. If one wants to achieve something in life, one has invested something on this behalf. Even though a drop of water barely makes a mark on the rock, the continuous dripping will make a hole on rock. An instantaneous success is a daydream and never exists in the history of mankind. 'If you want a success in your life, you have to have the wisdom of investment in yourself.' Schooling is one sure way to pave your road to success and there are many schools that one can attend to. Being an apprentice to a stonecutter is one of school that one can attend or being a student of sculptor is another school that one can attend. The main theme of schooling is staying long enough to learn the essential skill that one is after to get. It took me fifty years to get the fundamental skills in kendo and kendo also taught me what humble means in my life. Think ahead and invest something for your days to come. The most rewarding investment is investment for yourself.

The Last Letters 5 minutes permitting

18
가장 큰 수익을 얻으려면 자신에게 투자해라

Invest in yourself if you want a big return.

천리 길의 여행도 한 발짝으로 시작되고, 로마 역시 하루아침에 이루어지지 않았습니다. 무엇을 이루길 원한다면 반드시 투자가 있어야 하는 법. 한 방울의 물은 돌에 자국을 남기지 않지만, 계속해서 떨어지면 돌에 구멍을 만듭니다. 순간적인 성공은 있을 수 있지만 공중누각과 같아서 금세 허물어집니다. '인생에서 성공하려면 반드시 자신에 대한 투자를 할 줄 아는 지혜가 필요합니다.' 세상에는 많은 종류의 학교가 있지요. 넓게 보십시오. 돌을 다듬는 석공의 제자가 되거나, 조각가의 제자가 되는 것도 모두 학교가 됩니다. 중요한 건 학교에 들어가 충분히 오랫동안 공부해서 완벽하게 내 것으로 만드는 것입니다. 나는 검도와 기본을 얻는 데 50년이 소요되었고, 이를 통해서 겸손을 몸으로 배웠습니다. 미리 생각해서 내일은 무엇을 배울 것인가를 생각하고, 늘 자신을 위해서 투자하는 것이 가장 많은 것을 돌려받을 수 있는 지름길임을 꼭 기억하십시오!

Sniff, scurry, hem and haw are the four characters in a book named as "Who moved my cheese?" The theme of this book is CHANGE and this book tells us what we have to do in the time of change in our days on earth. Nothing is permanent and we have to be ready for the unexpected change that we have to face in future. The first thing for us to learn is our willingness to change in changing situation rather than fighting against the change. 'The second Law of Thermodynamics tells us that the natural processes have a direction such that the natural processes have no way of going against this direction.' If one process wants its own way to go, this process has to pay something. This may be the end of this process, i.e., this process never happens in nature. The same logic can be applied to us. If we can not change according to the change, we might get extinct from the world we live in. The second thing for us to learn is making preparations for the coming day. How do we prepare for the coming days? Be interested in the world around you and people of all walks of life. This will tell you where the change is heading for. Read much on all subjects and think much on what you read. This will give you a holistic view of the change. Thus you can enjoy the change when it comes to you in future.

The Last Letters 5 minutes permitting

19
영원히 변하지 않는 법칙은 세상은 바뀐다는 것이다

The unchanged law of the universe is change.

스님(냄새를 맡는 것), 스커리(빨리 왔다 갔다 하는 일), 햄과 호(심사숙고하는 것)는 『누가 내 치즈를 옮겼을까?』란 책의 네 명의 주인공입니다. 이 책의 주제는 변화로, 당장 내일의 변화에 어떻게 대처해야 하는지를 알려줍니다. 그 해법으로 변화와 싸우기보다는 변화를 따라 변하려는 의지를 제시합니다. '열역학 제2법칙은 자연계의 변화는 방향성이 있게 변하고, 어떠한 경우도 그 방향을 되돌릴 수 없음을 알려줍니다.' 만약 방향을 바꾸게 하려면 반드시 대가를 치러야 합니다. 이 말은 다시 말해서 자연계에 반하는 일은 절대로 그냥 일어나지 않는다는 말이죠. 이 논리는 우리의 삶에도 통용됩니다. 우리가 변화에 따라 변화하지 않으면 자동으로 소멸하게 된다는 이야기입니다. 그러므로 항상 깨어 있어 변화하는 미래를 준비해야 합니다. 총체적인 변화에 대해 알게 되면, 내일의 변화를 즐길 줄도 알게 됩니다.

A ship is seen passing in the horizo.
A fish passes in the deep sea.
Upon their passing, the sea is calm.

The sea named life many things come and go.
A deep cut, knotty problems, despair
and failure never stay with us permanently.
Nothing is permanent.

Someday the wind called time will drive them away.

모든 것은 변한다.
Nothing is permanent

수평선만 보이는 바다에 배 한 척이 지나간다.
깊이 모를 바다에 한 마리의 고기가 지나간다.
그들이 지나간 바다는 또다시 고요하다.

삶이라는 바다에도 많은 것들이 왔다 간다.
깊이 베인 상처, 풀지 않는 문제, 좌절, 실패······.
그러나 영원히 머무는 것은 없다.

언젠가는 시간의 바람이 그것들을 몰아간다.

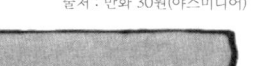

When you break with someone you loved, you are going to have a broken heart with much sorrow. Just imagine the coming days ahead with someone that you are going to love with all your heart. There are a lot of people who is willing to fall in love with you if a chance is given to them and you do let go of things that you could not hold as yours. 'Bygones are bygones and we will never get hold them like chasing the wind.' God always gives us second chance on all matters of life and you just wait for your second chance to come. One thing you remember would be just keeping your efforts up in finding someone you are attracted to. It is easier said than done and action beats inaction on all matters.

Just do rather than just sit on your butt. Do work your butt off on your chasing.

The Last Letters 5 minutes permitting

20
세상에는 많은 종류의 사람이 있다

There are a lot of people in the world.

사랑하는 사람과 헤어지게 되면 슬픔으로 가슴앓이를 하게 됩니다. 그러나 내일은 진정으로 사랑하게 될 새로운 사람이 나타날 거라고 상상해봅시다. 이 세상에는 사랑에 빠질 사람이 너무나 많이 있습니다. '지나간 일은 바람처럼 잡지 못하니 어제는 어제로 치부하십시오.' 하나님은 우리에게 제2의 기회를 주시기에 이 제2의 기회를 기다리십시다. 그렇더라도 스스로 사랑하는 사람을 찾는 노력은 해야 합니다. 말하기는 쉬워도 행동에 옮기기는 쉽지 않지요.
그냥 가만히 앉아 있지만 말고, 열심히 내가 원하는 사람을 쫓아다니는 노력을 하십시오.

Unskilled carpenter might blame his tools rather than his poor skills in his carpentry works. The blind might blame the ditch by the same token. Passing the buck to others is the inherent nature of human being. Theodore Roosevelt, the 26th president of the United States, showed us this inherent buck passing human nature could be corrected. During his presidency he put a sign on his desk, the sign goes, "The buck stops here." In other words, it is I not you who are responsible on all mishaps. Everyday we meet and do many things and all things do not turn up right all the time. It is our attitudes toward all things that really count in our lives rather than the results. 'Do act like you are the one that blame has to go, not your neighbors on all mishaps of your life.' The peace of the world can be restored through not passing the buck to others. Do say praiseworthy remarks toward your neighbors on their good deeds.

The Last Letters 5 minutes permitting

21
앞을 못 보는 사람이라면 개울을 원망하지 말아라

If you are blind, do not blame the ditch.

일에 서툰 목수는 자신의 기술 부족보다 연장을 원망하고, 마찬가지로 앞을 못 보는 사람은 개울을 원망합니다. 일이 잘못되면 항상 남의 탓으로 돌리는 것은 인간의 타고난 본성입니다. 이런 맥락에서 미국의 26대 대통령 테오도르 루스벨트는 남의 탓으로 돌리는 나쁜 습성을 어떻게 방지할 수 있는지를 보여주었습니다. 대통령이 되면서 자신의 책상에 "모든 책임은 궁극적으로 나에게 있다."는 팻말을 놓아두었지요. 쉽게 풀이하면 모든 힘든 문제는 대통령인 자신이 해결한다는 이야기입니다. 날마다 일어나는 모든 일들이 항상 잘될 수만은 없습니다. 그러나 어떻게 마음먹느냐에 따라서 결과와는 무관하게 다르게 느낄 수 있습니다. '잘못되면 남이 아니라 내게 모든 책임이 있다는 마음을 가지십시오.' 세상의 평화는 잘못을 남에게 넘기지 않을 때, 또한 이웃의 선행이 칭찬으로 이어질 때 만들어집니다.

If one gives you piggy back, you want to go on horseback. Give you an inch, you will take a mile. Our desire knows no bound and every act of our lives leave much to be desired due to our greed. In nature a mountain has the highest peak and a river has a source along with its final destination. Human is the only creature that does not satisfy on what they have at present. This unbound desire for things was the source of human development but the happiness of an individual is heavily relied on the greed that each individual has. The more one has, the more one wants until one gets sick on one's greed. Having a lot of material goods gives one much freedom and at the same time it gives one much headache.

The road to happiness should not be paved with material goods but paved with the peace of mind. 'How do we achieve the peace of mind? Disciplining our mind is one way and learning the prayer of thanksgiving on all matters that we face in our journey on life is another.' Do meditate on your beginning along with ending so that you can put a lid on your desire for your happy days.

The Last Letters 5 minutes permitting

22
아무리 많은 구경을 해도 우리의 눈은 만족을 모른다

Our eyes can never see enough
to be satisfied.

누군가가 당신을 업어준다면 다음에는 말이 타고 싶어질 것입니다. 한 뼘을 주면 당신은 오 리(2km)를 원할 것입니다. 이처럼 모든 일에 만족을 못 하는 이유는 탐욕 때문입니다. 산은 최고의 봉우리가 있고, 강은 근원지와 끝이 있습니다. 하지만 인간만이 자기가 가진 현재의 것에 만족을 하지 못합니다. 끝이 없는 욕망이 인류를 발전시키는 원동력이 되었지만, 개인이 느끼는 행복은 욕망과 반비례합니다. 이 욕망이라는 것은 병이 날 때까지 계속 이어집니다. 많이 가진다는 것은 자유도 주지만, 또한 머리도 아프게 합니다. 행복은 마음의 평화로 얻어지지 물질적인 것으로 이룰 수 없습니다. 그러면 '어떻게 마음의 평화를 얻을까요? 첫째, 우리의 마음을 길들입시다. 둘째, 모든 일에 감사기도를 합시다.' 참선을 통해 욕망의 뚜껑을 덮으십시오. 영원한 행복을 위해서 말입니다.

The bird in its flight does not leave a mark
when it reaches to its destination.
The boiling water is willing to change its shape.

The beauty of detachment is that it does not leave a mark.

흔적을 남기지 않는다
does not leave a mark

독수리가 날아갈 때
The flight of an eagle

흔적을 남기지 않는 것이 현명한 삶이다
No mark or no trace is the wise way of living.

새는 흔적을 남기지 않고도 가고자 하는 곳으로 가고

끓는 물은 제 모양을 고집하지 않는다.

초월의 모습이 아름다운 것은 자취를 남기지 않기 때문이다.

물방울도 끓는 물 속에서 흔적을 남기지 않는다.
Neither do the bubbles in boiling water

출처 : 만화 30원(야스미디어)

When you learn to walk, you are ready to run. Life always gives you things to learn for your days to come. If we want a toughened iron bar, we have to do many tempering on an iron bar. Thus the same is true in making a tough mind optimist Tough problems of life give us a chance to toughen our body and mind. Tough problems also offer us an opportunity to grow. Our views on life will be enlarged through our growth and we can have better chance to do things better.

In life we have to learn to turn the stumbling block of our lives into the stepping stone such that in the end we become the winners in life. 'Do not fear tough problems in life. Problems in life are the blessings in disguised when we tackle the problems and get over with them.' If we can not tackle the problems in life, you have to learn to pray for our problems. A big problem needs a bigger prayer of ours to be solved. Be happy when we have knotty problems to solve. This problem will give us a new dimension for our coming days.

The Last Letters 5 minutes permitting

23
아무 문제없는 삶에서는 더 이상의 성장도 없다

Grow from your problem.

강한 철로 된 몽둥이를 원한다면 철 몽둥이를 계속해서 담금질해야 합니다. 같은 원리로 강한 긍정의 마음 역시 담금질하는 과정이 필요합니다. 피하고 싶은 인생의 힘든 문제가 바로 우리를 성장시킵니다. 힘든 일을 겪고 성장하면 마음도 크게 되어 일도 더 잘할 수 있습니다. 그러므로 우리 앞에 높은 바윗덩어리가 버티면 더 높이 도약할 수 있는 징검다리로 삼아야 합니다. 그래서 기필코 승자로 자리매김해야 합니다. '힘든 문제를 겁내지 마십시오. 힘든 문제 이면에 축복이 기다리고 있습니다.' 만약 스스로 힘든 문제를 해결하지 못한다면 기도하는 법을 배워야 합니다. 힘든 문제는 기도로 해결될 수 있습니다. 지금 당신에게 너무나 힘든 문제가 있나요? 그렇다면 먼저 감사기도부터 올리시지요.

When one asks you a helping hand, lend him your assistance. A river of financial problem, a river of physical problem, a river of mental problem, and many kinds of rivers have to be crossed in our lives. Sometimes we need a boat to cross a river of some kind of difficulty in our lives, but a timely boat is hard to find. If we want to enjoy a full blossom of flowers, we have to plant a flowering plant beforehand. If you want to get a helping hand in days to come, you have to lend many helping hands to the needy when you can. Nothing comes free in life and we get what we put into our lives. 'A life is like a boomerang. If we give or lend good things toward the needy or the poor, we will get the same things in return.' Be a boat for those rivers to cross and enjoy the good feelings coming from the beyond. Then we are in the heart of God and our heart becomes God.

The Last Letters 5 minutes permitting

24
강을 건너야 할 사람에게 배가 되어 주어라

Become a boat for those
rivers to cross.

누군가가 도움을 청하면 도와주십시오. 인생은 건너야 할 강이 많이 있습니다. 경제적으로 건너야 할 강, 육체적으로 건너야 할 강, 정신적으로 건너야 할 강 등등.

가끔씩 꼭 건너야 하는데 어려운 문제의 강도 있습니다. 하지만 그럴 때 유용한 배를 찾기란 쉽지 않지요. 꽃의 만개를 즐기려면 미리 심어야 하듯이, 미래에 도움을 받고 싶다면 도와줄 수 있는 여력이 있을 때 많이 도와주시오. '삶은 부메랑과 같아서, 좋은 것을 힘든 이에게 나누어주면, 언젠가 같은 것을 돌려받을 수 있습니다.' 강을 건너야 되는 사람에게 배가 되어 주어 베푸는 즐거움과 행복을 즐기십시오. 그 순간이야말로 하나님의 품안에서 우리의 가슴이 하나님이 되는 순간입니다.

출처 : 나눔그림 (아름다운 재단, 콩반쪽)

봄이 아직 어린
어린 아기 나눔이
우리 곁에 풍성한
씨알의 나눔의 숲으로
약속합니다.

In the book titled, "The Present." Author gives us a real important message, namely we have to live in the present. Thus we have to learn from the past and we are going to program for our days to come. What does it mean to live in the present? Living in the present can be expressed in the following analogy. When we ride a car, we become a car. When we read a book, we become a book. 'In doing something, we become the thing we do. Living in the present also tells us that we do one thing at a time with all our mind and body.' We worry about the future that has not come yet and we do not know whether it will come or not. We go over the bygone days and we daydream about what if we did this or that on the past events. There is a saying, "Let bygones be bygones." We can do nothing on the past and it is better to forget about it. Do learn to live in the present and have wonders of life. Live now what others will only live in the future.

The Last Letters 5 minutes permitting

25
현재에 살아라

Being in the present.

『현재』라는 책을 쓴 저자는 현재에 산다는 것이 무엇이고 왜 중요한지 일깨워줍니다. 그에 따르면 어제의 일에서 교훈을 찾고 내일을 계획하며 살아야 한다고 이야기합니다. 현재에 산다는 것은 무슨 의미일까요? 예를 들어보지요.

만약 현재 차를 타고 있다면 나는 차가 되고, 현재 책을 읽고 있다면 나는 책이 되어버리는 일입니다. 즉 '객체와 내가 하나가 되어 녹아버리는 것이죠. 또한 현재에 산다는 것은 한순간에 한 가지 일에만 열중한다는 의미도 포함되어 있습니다.' 오지도 않는 내일을 걱정하면서 시간을 허비하지 마십시오. 내일은 오지 않을 수도 있습니다. 또한 어제는 지나간 날이기에 잊어버려야 합니다. 현재에 살면서 멋진 삶을 즐기시지요. 남이 내일에 산다면 나는 현재에 살겠습니다.

We get a chance to succeed in life if we are ready to grab the chance given to us. Opportunity for success in life is given to all but some can make it happen. If we want a healthy body, we have to plan to spend some hours in the gym. If one wants to be a curator of a gallery, one has to see many paintings such that one can tell a painting is genuine or fake. It takes time and efforts for us to be good at something but we are not willing to invest our time and efforts in achieving meaningful thing in life. We are more apt to get the quick results rather than wait something meaningful that needs time and efforts to mature. Life is a long journey and we need to have patience to wait for a thing to be matured enough for us to get. 'It takes ten months to give birth to a baby but it takes our whole life to raise our kids to maturity. Learn to wait and be prepared for the meaningful thing in life.'

The Last Letters 5 minutes permitting

26
기회는 준비된 자에게만 주어진다

A chance is given to the prepared one.

기회가 올 때 기회를 잡을 수 있는 준비가 되어 있다면 반드시 성공적인 인생을 살 것입니다. 누구에게나 기회는 주어집니다만, 성공하는 사람은 정해져 있지요? 건강해지려면 일정 시간을 체육관에서 보내야 하고, 박물관 큐레이터가 되고 싶다면 수많은 그림을 보고 진품 여부를 판단할 수 있어야 합니다. 전문가가 되려면 많은 시간과 노력이 필요함을 알지만, 노력은 안 하고 빠른 결실만 얻기를 원합니다. 인생은 긴 여행길입니다. '아기는 이 세상에 나오기 위해 열 달을 엄마 뱃속에서 꼬박 보내야 합니다. 그렇듯이 준비하고 기다릴 줄 아는 인내심을 기릅시다.'

"Be ready for your opportunity when it comes."

기회가 왔을 때에는 준비가 되어 있어야 한다.

- Benjamin Disraeli -

'A rosy life is a fantasy we might have in our dreams. Living a life is not an easy job for all of us.' Sometimes we might hit a bump and this might give us blues hard to shake off. Life has to be lived even if we are not willing to. If we have no alternatives on matters we face in life, we have to find ways to deal with this knotty matter. Blues give us the down days and we have to learn to shake off our blues in our lives. One might find consolation just listening to music that one likes. Another finds it in sports. Mountain climbing might be one solution and trekking the Himalayan treks might be another. There are many ways to skin a cat so the ways to shake off the blues are many. Find ways to shake off our blues are the ways to be happy in our lives on earth.

The Last Letters 5 minutes permitting

27
빨리 우울함을 떨치는 법을 익혀라

Learn to shake off blues of life.

'장밋빛 인생은 꿈속에서나 존재하는 환상입니다. 산다는 것은 고행입니다.' 가끔은 장애물에 부딪히고, 그럴 때마다 떨칠 수 없는 우울감에 빠지기 일쑤입니다. 내 힘으로는 어떻게 해볼 도리가 없기에 더 우울해지고 기운이 빠집니다. 하지만 이 우울함을 빨리 떨쳐버려야 합니다. 어떻게 떨쳐버릴 수 있을까요? 음악을 듣든, 운동을 하든, 히말라야 트래킹에 도전하든 빨리 우울함의 늪에서 빠져나와야 합니다. 우울함을 떨치는 방법도 여러 가지입니다. 여러 길을 모색해서 행복한 삶을 사십시오.

It is far easier saying a thing than doing a thing. Action is harder than inaction. It might be our human nature that speak much and do little. It is wise saying little and doing much in the day-to-day activities of ours. Even though our imagination is larger than the world around us, we have to put a lid on our bragging on all matters of life. There is a saying, "It is easier said than done." This saying tells us the faulty nature of human being. Let us speak little on what we have achieved and do more in doing good things to needy and the poor such that our days on earth do not make any disturbance on life itself. 'Wisdom of life can be gained through thinking much and doing wise activities much, not through speaking much.'

The Last Letters 5 minutes permitting

28
적게 말하고 많이 행동해라

Speak little, do much.

말하기는 쉬워도 행동으로 옮기기는 힘듭니다. 실천보다 말만 앞서는 것은 어쩌면 인간의 본성입니다. 말은 행동보다 쉽다는 속담이 있는데 이 속담은 인간의 약점을 여실히 드러내줍니다. 의식적으로 말은 적게 하고 행동을 많이 하도록 합시다. 특히 힘든 이에게 평소 베푸는 연습을 합시다. '지혜란, 말은 적게 하고 많이 생각하고, 현명한 일들을 많이 함으로써 얻어집니다.'

In lifer's adventure one has to concentrate one thing at a time if one wants to make oner's life successful. When one goes on a fishing trip, one has to think about fishing related things all through oner's trip. In classroom we have to think about what we are learning. Doing one thing at a time with all your might will be the way to success. 'We are programmed to do a thing at a time and just stick to this simple rule for our survival. One cannot beat a drum and perform a dance at the same time.' One beats a drum and another performs a dance are the logical process in everyday life. Keep in mind that we can do something better when we do a thing at a time. Many tried doing many things in a given time but a few did succeed since we are born to be winner in one specific thing in our lives. God gives us a chance to find one thing we are entitled to have but we miss the target by trying many things in a given time. When you sit, just sit for your own good in life.

The Last Letters 5 minutes permitting

29
앉아야 할 때는 앉는 것에만 신경을 써라

When you sit, just sit.

성공하고 싶은가요? 미련하게 굴지 말고 한 번에 한 가지 일에만 열중하면 됩니다. 물고기를 잡으러 가면 물고기 잡는 일에만 신경을 집중해야 하고, 학교에 가면 배우는 일에만 신경을 집중해야 합니다. 한 번에 한 가지 일에만 집중하는 것이 성공하는 길임을 잊지 맙시다. '인간으로 태어난 이상 한 번에 한 가지 일에만 집중하는 것이 최선의 방책이고, 이것이 생존의 법칙입니다. 북 치고 장구 치는 일을 동시에 할 수 없다는 말입니다.' 한 사람이 북을 치면, 다른 한 사람은 춤추는 것이 일의 순서입니다. 또한 기억해야 할 것은, 한 번에 한 가지 일을 할 때 더 잘할 수 있다는 사실입니다. 많은 사람이 주어진 시간 안에 많은 일을 하려 하지만 적은 수의 사람만 성공하는 이유는 인간인 이상 한 가지 일에서만 성공하게 되어 있기 때문입니다. 하나님은 우리가 한 가지 일에 매진할 때 성공할 수 있는 기회를 주시는데도 우리는 여러 가지 일을 한꺼번에 하려다 모든 기회를 놓치고 맙니다. 앉아야 할 때는 앉는 일에만 온 신경을 집중하십시오.

The cactuses can be rotten if you water them every day.
A fish car't live in a dishful of water.
You can't go far with heavy loads on your back.
Sometimes light loads make you lazy.

The extreme measure is the cul-de-sac in life
and you will go most safely in the middle.

물이 너무 많다
Too much water

물이 너무 적다
Too little water

중용의 도
Moderation

선인장을 너무 아껴 매일 물을 주면 선인장은 썩어간다.
몸도 채 잠기지 않는 접시 물에서 물고기가 살아갈 수는 없다.
욕심껏 진 짐은 걷지 못하게 다리를 꺾고
너무 가벼운 짐은 정신의 나태를 부른다.

극단은 더 나아갈 수 없는 막다른 골목과 같다.
중용의 도는 가장 적당한 생의 무게중심이다.

너무 무겁다
Too heavy

너무 가볍다
Too light

출처 : 만화 30원(야스미디어)

In the middle of crisis one has to think that the crisis will be over in the end because the beginning contains the ending in the way a closing opens a new starting. 'Life consists of symmetric events such that a sunny day can not exist without a rainy day.' An uphill does give us downhill at the end and so does a tough problem with a good ending. One has to remain positive even if one faces a big crisis in one's life since everything changes as time flows. 'Nothing is permanent. Everlasting change is the only thing that stays true.' There is a saying, "After a storm comes calm." After we go through a crisis, we become strong because a crisis strengthens us our mind and body. Just remember that everything that has a beginning has an ending such that we can face the rainy days with positive mental attitude for our days to come. Everything that goes up must come down and a peak will be a valley in the coming days.

The Last Letters 5 minutes permitting

30
모든 일은 시작이 있으면 끝이 있다

Everything that has a beginning has an ending.

지금 위기의 순간이라면 한 가지만 기억합시다. "모든 일이 시작이 있으면 끝이 있다." 왜냐하면 시작은 끝을 포함하고 있기 때문입니다. '삶은 대칭성을 띠고 있기에 햇빛 나는 날도 비오는 날이 없으면 존재하지 않습니다.' 마찬가지로 오르막길은 내리막길이 없이 존재하지 않고, 그러므로 힘든 문제는 좋은 결실을 포함하고 있다는 말입니다. '모든 일이 변하기에 아무리 힘든 순간이 와도 우리는 긍정적으로 남아 있어야 합니다. 정말 모든 것은 변합니다.' "폭풍우 뒤에 고요가 온다."는 말이 있습니다. 위기를 겪은 뒤에 더 강해지는 법입니다. 모든 일에 시작이 있으면 끝이 있음을 생각하고, 힘든 시기를 긍정적으로 생각하고 내일을 맞이해야 합니다. 올라간 것은 내려오게 되어 있고, 오늘의 산꼭대기는 내일에는 골짜기가 된다는 것도 기억하십시오.

We are the architect of our lives and have to struggle to make the life we want to have. 'There are many turns and stumbling block to create the path we want to follow in our lives. Many trials and errors will be our teachers in making the life we want to create.' An artist has to practice unlimited number of trials before being recognized as an artist and so is the life we want to create. We have to try many trials and pave many paths to find the path we eagerly want to pave in our lives. Just give all we can in finding and searching the path we want to create such that our lives will have meaning of our existence. There is more than one path that we have to pave in our lives. Paving more paths is blissful since we may feel and enjoy the varieties of walks of life. Always we have the right to enjoy the path we have taken and we have to prepare enjoying the moment we have right now.

The Last Letters 5 minutes permitting

31
내 운명을 스스로 창조해라

Create your own destiny.

내 운명을 만드는 건축가는 나입니다. 원하는 삶을 살기 위해 행운을 바라거나 남에게 기대지 맙시다. 스스로 만들어야 합니다. '원하는 것을 창조하기 위해서는 많은 길을 돌아가야 하고 또한 많은 장애를 넘어야 합니다. 수많은 시행착오는 인생의 선생님입니다.' 가령 예술가는 예술가로 인정받기까지 얼마나 많은 시행착오를 거칩니까? 우리 역시 원하는 삶을 창조하기 위해서 똑같은 노력이 필요합니다. 여러 길을 섭렵해야 하고 많은 시도를 해야만 진정 원하는 길을 찾을 수 있습니다. 우리의 인생은 한 가지 길만 있는 것은 아닙니다. 만약 한 길이 아닌 여러 길을 섭렵할 수 있다면 큰 은총입니다. 왜냐하면 그만큼 많은 종류의 삶을 느낄 수 있기 때문입니다. 항상 우리는 우리가 택한 길을 즐길 권리가 있고, 또한 우리가 택한 길을 즐길 수 있도록 늘 준비되어 있어야겠지요.

"Do what you love, the money will follow."

당신이 좋아하는 입을 하면, 돈은 따라온다.

- Marsha Sinetar -

During our days on earth we may have a day when we have to burn our bridge for our survival. If one knows that there is no way but to fight off the problem, one can have a big chance to win. It is our attitude that makes us winner or loser in a game called life. How many deaths do we have to face in our lives?

One death is what we are going to have in our own lives. When one meets an obstacle that is too big to tackle, one has to find many alternatives to go over the obstacle; Going through the obstacle, going under the obstacle, smashing the obstacle or going over the obstacle. It is our frame of mind that determines the output of all matters in life. 'When we meet the limit of our ability in solving the problems of our lives, we have only one solution and burning our bridge is one and the only solution for the problem.'

The Last Letters 5 minutes permitting

32
배수의 진을 쳐라

Burn your bridge behind you.

막다른 골목에서 살아남기 위해 배수의 진을 쳐야 할 때가 있습니다. 싸우는 길만이 유일한 해결책이라면 싸움에 이길 수 있습니다. 모든 일이 우리의 태도에 따라서 삶이란 놀이에서 승자나 패자로 결정됩니다. 살아가면서 얼마나 많은 죽음을 맞이하시겠습니까?

단 한 번의 죽음만 맞이하십시다. 나의 능력으로 해결하기 역부족인 문제는 때로는 여우처럼 다른 방법으로 해결해야 합니다. 장애물을 통과해서 가든지, 장애물 밑으로 살짝 수그려 가든지, 넘어서 가든지 또는 장애물을 깨부수고 가든지 여러 방법 중 적합한 방법으로 해결하면 됩니다. '모든 것이 마음의 문제입니다. 해결할 수 없는 문제는 배수의 진을 치면 해결이 가능합니다.'

If you want to stand firmly on the ground, you need two legs. Also on a cold night, two men under the same blanket gain warmth from each other. Two men can accomplish more than twice as much as one man. A double-braided cord is easily broken than a triple-braided cord. Thus two is better than one. In lifer's journey we need many helpers to achieve our goals in life and also we have to learn to be good helpers for the needy and the poor. In singing, a duet is better than a solo since each singer has to learn to harmonize with his or her partner.

'Let us learn the beauty of harmony through keeping the phrase that two is better than one. If we cooperate with someone on something, it adds music to our work and to our lives.'

The Last Letters 5 minutes permitting

33
둘이 하나보다 좋다

Two is better than one.

땅에 안정되게 서 있으려면 두 다리가 필요하고, 아주 추운 날에는 두 사람이 함께 담요 밑에 누워 있으면 서로의 따스함으로 추위를 이길 수 있습니다. 한편 두 겹으로 꼬인 밧줄은 세 겹으로 꼬인 밧줄보다 쉽게 끊어집니다. 삶이란 여행에서 우리는 많은 이들의 도움을 받아서 목표를 이룹니다. 그러므로 받은 도움을 돈 없고 힘든 이에게 베풀어야 합니다.

'둘이 하나보다 좋다는 명제를 가지고 조화를 배웁시다. 혼자 노래 부를 때보다 화음을 맞춰야 하듯이.'

"My joy in giving is greater than yours in receiving."

당신이 받는 기쁨보다, 내가 주는 기쁨이 더 크다.

- Louis H. Severance,

Founder of Severance Hospital of Yonsei Univ. -

The best way to handle our fear is to face it rather than avoid it. Most of things we fear in life do not appear in our lives and we worry away our days worrying about our fear. Like thing attracts like thing. If we think of something scaring, we are going to get it as the result of our thinking. Let us change our ways of thinking and do have happy and blessed days. Learn the simple wisdom of life. 'It might go, Practice makes perfect.' Just practice a new of thinking on worries and throw away our unnecessary worries on life for our better days to come.

The Last Letters 5 minutes permitting

34
두려움은 피하지 말고 직접 부딪혀라

Beat fear through facing it.

두려움을 극복하는 가장 좋은 방법은 무엇일까요? 피하기보다 직접 마주하는 것입니다. 실제로 우리 삶에서 두려워하는 많은 일들은 일어나지 않는데도 미리 걱정으로 귀한 세월을 보냅니다. 같은 것은 같은 것을 끌어당기는 법이지요. 무엇을 무서워하면, 그 생각이 그 무서운 것을 끌어들여서 현실로 나타나게 합니다. 생각의 틀을 바꾸어야 행복한 축복을 누릴 수 있습니다. '오직 연습만이 완벽함을 만든다는 간단한 진리를 다시 되새깁시다.' 쓸모없는 걱정일랑 떨쳐버리고 다가오는 날만을 맞이하십시다.

"Worry empties today of its joy."

걱정은 오늘의 기쁨을 삼켜버린다.

- Anonymous -

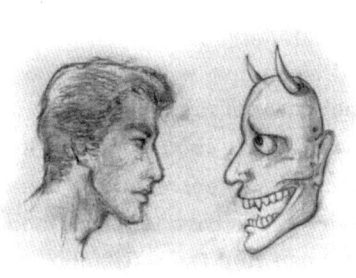

'One can find a paradise in hell and also can find a hell in paradise.' One's state of mind will create both, i.e., paradise and hell. One dollar is enough money for the poor of the poorest to live a day, whereas it is a mere pittance for the have. The desire of the have to amass money has no bound and they never can find the satisfaction they have wanted. There is the highest peak of a mountain, but there is no peak for one's desire. Set our limit on our desires and we will find our blessings coming from the state of our mind.

The Last Letters 5 minutes permitting

35
가난은 내 마음의 상태이다
Poor is your state of mind.

'어떤 사람은 지옥에서 천국을 발견할 수 있고, 또 어떤 사람은 천국에서 지옥을 발견할 수 있습니다.' 일 달러의 돈은 가장 가난한 나라의 사람에게는 하루를 보낼 수 있는 돈이지만, 가진 자에게는 아무것도 아닙니다. 가진 자가 돈을 많이 벌겠다는 욕망에는 끝이 없고 만족이란 것을 결코 모릅니다. 세상에 가장 높은 산봉우리는 있어도, 욕망의 끝은 없습니다. 그러니 욕망에 족쇄를 채우십시오. 그 순간 마음에서 오는 은총을 발견할 것입니다.

Do concentrate on what you do
as if you can't perceive your existence.

You will experience the ecstasy of samadhi.
Your concentration will change your attitude
and save you from the slump of yours.
You will get more than you expect.

출처 : 만화 30원 (야스미디어)

당신은 지금 어디에 있는가?
Where are you?

하고 있는 일에 열중해보자.
자신을 잊어버릴 만큼.

삼매의 황홀경을 경험하게 될 것이다.
그 집중은 당신을 변화시키고 슬럼프에서 일으키며
기대 이상의 결과물을 안겨줄 것이다.

Our dream will never be actualized without starting to do something to achieve it.

Sea is made of collection of water drops and so is mountain through piling up earth. It is easy to daydream a thing but it is not an easy job to begin it. 'Thinking is one thing and doing is another thing in life. When we think about something new, we have to think hard how to do the thing we have thought over.' If we want to catch fish, we have to go to sea or river to catch it. If we want water in the desert, we have to dig deep to get it. In life nothing is free and if we want to get something, we are willing to pay for it. A big tower is started with one brick and so is The Great Wall of China. Lefs do something rather than wait if we really wish to achieve something in our lives. Remember that if we shoot for the moon, we might land at the top of the highest mountain. Just begin the thing we want to achieve in our lives rather than waste our lives. Do not wait so long to begin works of ours because we can not buy time.

The Last Letters 5 minutes permitting

36
중요한 것은 어떻게든 시작하는 일이다

The important thing is somehow to begin.

꿈은 지금 바로 시작하지 않는 한 결코 이룰 수가 없습니다. 바다는 물방울이 모여서, 산은 흙이 모여서 만들어진 것입니다. 몽상하기는 쉽지만 몽상한 일을 행동으로 행하는 일은 쉽지 않습니다. '생각하는 일은 이 생각을 행동으로 실행하는 것과는 천지차이입니다. 만약 새로운 일을 생각하면, 어떻게 이 새로운 일을 실행하는가를 심각하게 생각해야 합니다.' 고기를 잡길 원한다면, 빨리 바다나 강으로 가야 합니다. 사막에서 물이 나오길 원하면 깊게 땅을 파서 얻어야 합니다. 세상에는 공짜가 없어서 무엇을 원하면 원하는 것을 위해서 그에 합당한 대가를 치러야 합니다. 높은 탑도 한 개의 돌에서 시작했고, 만리장성도 이와 같습니다. 무엇이라도 이루려면 기다리지 말고 당장 일을 시작합시다. 만약 달을 목표로 삼았다면, 적어도 산꼭대기라도 도달하지 않겠습니까? 원하는 일이 있다면, 그냥 시작하시지요. 너무 오래 기다리지 마십시오. 시간은 살 수 없습니다.

If one wants to be a champion in a game, one has to play for the championship. If one wants to be a writer, one has to submit one's manuscripts to publishers. The rule of success is to act more aggressively rather than defensively. 'If the opportunity does not knock one's door, one has to make a door to be knocked.' If there isn't a road to reach one's destination, one has to make a road for that purpose. Opportunity is looking for the one who is willing to grab it rather than a lazybones. There is a saying, "Heaven helps those who help themselves." One has to struggle or fight for the success if one wants the final trophy of success. The prepared has more chance for success since he or she is willing to go extra miles for success and have the alertness for the opportunity for success. Do things more aggressive alertness for success. One will climb all steps of opportunity if one builds a door that has to be knocked.

The Last Letters 5 minutes permitting

37
기회가 노크하지 않으면 노크할 수 있게 문을 만들어라

Build a door if opportunity does not knock.

챔피언이 되려면 피나는 연습을 해야 합니다. 작가가 되려면 출판사에 원고를 넘겨야 합니다. 성공의 비법은 보다 공격적으로 노력함에 있습니다. '만약 기회가 노크를 하지 않으면, 문을 만들어서라도 노크하게 해야 합니다.' 만약 목적지로 가는 길이 없으면 만들어야 합니다. 기회는 기회를 붙잡으려는 사람을 기다리고 부지런하지 않은 사람을 기다리지 않습니다. 속담에 하늘은 스스로 돕는 자를 돕는다고 했지요. 최후의 승리라는 트로피를 원하면 싸워야 합니다. 준비된 자는 성공을 위해서 더 노력하는 마음을 가지고 있고 성공을 위한 기회를 항상 기다립니다. 성공을 위해서 좀 더 공격적인 행동을 취합시다. 노크할 문을 만드는 사람은 기회를 모두 잡을 것입니다.

When one wants to create a path of one's own liking in life, one has to make many turns and overcome many obstacles. It is the way of life and we are willing to make turns if we have to. There is a saying, "A shortcut is a losing cut." A shortcut may lead us the path to our downfall like becoming famous overnight. A real success does not happen overnight and so does the creation of famous art works. It takes time and efforts to make something valuable and we also meet many difficulties along the way. A bend in life gives us a new chance to challenge.

Also it gives us a new frame of mind about the thing we create. 'Thus those who do not give up easily will get the rewards at the end of their work. Make the bend in the road into blessings through unlimited struggling and have the wonder of life at the end.'

The Last Letters 5 minutes permitting

38
가는 길이 힘들다고 해서 길의 끝이 아니다

A bend in the road is not
the end of the road.

원하는 인생을 살기 위해 많이 돌아갈 수도 있고 수없는 장애물을 넘어야만 가능할 수 있습니다. 억울해하지 마십시오. 이것이 삶의 길이며, 그래서 돌아가야 한다면 돌아가야 합니다. 지름길이 망하는 길이라는 속담이 있습니다. 지름길은 하룻밤 사이에 성공을 맛보게 하지만 곧 패망의 길로 인도합니다. 진짜 성공은 절대 하룻밤 만에 이루어지지 않습니다. 위대한 예술작품도 이와 같지 않습니까? 어떤 일이 귀하게 되는 과정에 는 반드시 시간과 노력이 필요합니다. 많은 장애를 넘어야 합니다. 가는 길이 험하면 도전의 기회를 줍니다. 그리고 새로운 마음의 틀도 줍니다. '쉽게 포기하지 않는 자만이 끝에는 노력의 대가를 받습니다. 가는 길이 험하다는 것이 축복이 되어서 많은 투쟁 뒤에는 삶의 은총을 받아야 합니다.'

"Take everything that comes along."

따라오는 대로 받아라.

- Ecclesiastes 7:8 -

"What goes up must come down."

산 넘어 산이다.

- American proverb -

When one goes on a trip, one has to have a destination in one's trip. We should have the reason to live for in our lives the way travelers seek their destination. 'God gives each of us a special talent such that through it we can enjoy our days on earth. These talents of ours can be the reason for living or means to reveal our real meaning of existence.'

When one thinks too much of reasons for living, one might confine oneself to a mental hospital and might lead a horrible life. A simple life leads us to better views on what to live for. Only a child can see that the emperor is naked as appeared in the children's storybook. Thus only an undisturbed mind will see thing clearly so that we can easily find the meaning of our existence, in other words the reason we live for in our lives. In meditation we strip ourselves completely such that the real core of ourselves will be revealed the way we see ourselves better in a clean mirror. Try hard to find the reason to live for and have a bountiful Life.

The Last Letters 5 minutes permitting

39
왜 살아야 하는지 이유가 있다

Do have the reason to live for.

여행을 떠날 때 목적지를 정하고 떠납니다. 우리의 삶도 목적지를 가지고 떠나는 여행처럼 사는 이유가 있어야 합니다. '하나님은 각자에게 삶을 즐길 수 있는 달란트를 주셨습니다. 이 달란트는 우리가 사는 이유일 수 있습니다.' 하지만 너무 존재의 의미에 매달려 집착하면 정신병동에 가서 살아야 할지도 모릅니다. 단순하게 살아가는 것이 정답일 수 있습니다. 어느 동화에서 임금님이 벌거벗었다는 것을 어린 아이가 알아내지 않습니까? 조용히 관조하는 삶이 우리가 사는 이유를 알려줄 것입니다. 참선하는 가운데 자신을 또렷이 잘 볼 수 있는 이유는 모든 것을 벗어던진 자신을 맑은 거울에서처럼 보기 때문입니다. 왜 사는가를 생각하고 풍요롭게 사십시오.

출처 : 만화 30원(야스미디어)

생중계 방송

운동중계 방송

음악중계 방송

뉴스 방송

죽음은?
what is the death?

죽음은 KBS TV를 보다가
MBC TV로 채널을 바꾸는 것과 같다.

The death is nothing but the changing of your T.V. station.
In other words, you switch your T.V. Channel from KBS to MBC.

If one wants to become a millionaire, one has to have a millionairess mind. If one wants to amass a fortune, one has to know that wealth is a result rather than a cause. It also reminds us of the fact that once one decides to make money, the decision has to be followed by actions related with making money. There is a saying "Money talks." Money has the power to do things and money has the power to make people do things. There are many ways to make money, i.e., pinching penny, saving through skipping meals, loan-sharking ...... etc.

The nutshell of making money is reminding one of the facts that the end account is what it counts rather than the beginning account the way we play games. 'One more fact to remember is that billionaires of the world amassed their fortune through serving the mass not exploiting them.' Thus one sure way of making money is to find the way to serve the mass and memorizing that wealth is a result rather than a cause.

The Last Letters 5 minutes permitting

40
돈을 모은다는 것은 단지 결과물이다

Wealth is a result.

백만장자가 되려면 백만장자의 마음을 가져야 합니다. 돈을 버는 것은 결과의 산물이지 어떤 이유의 산물은 아닙니다. 돈을 벌겠다고 결심했으면 그에 걸맞은 행동이 따라야 합니다. 돈이 말한다는 속담이 있습니다. 돈은 사람으로 하여금 어떤 일을 시키는 힘이 있습니다. 돈은 어떻게 벌 수 있을까요? 한 푼 두 푼 아끼고 밥을 굶고, 또는 고리대금업을 하든지······. 가지가지 방법이 다 있겠지요. '기억할 것은, 돈은 단지 결과물이라는 사실입니다. 또 한 가지 기억할 것은 지금껏 알려진 백만장자들은 많은 사람들에게 봉사함으로써 돈을 모았다는 사실입니다.' 결코 남의 등을 쳐서 돈을 모은 것이 아니라는 거죠. 많은 사람에게 봉사하다 보면 저절로 부자가 된다는 놀라운 비밀을 한번 믿어보시지요.

When we are involved in any projects, we aim for perfection. When we go to war against someone, we want a perfect victory. In other words we want 100% of everything. Sometimes achieving 51% of some job means success and 49% means failure. Many people want 100% gain on all things they are involved in and more often than not face the total failure. Our greedy nature is the source of all troubles and we have to learn practicing moderation on all matters in life. If one wants to enjoy delicious foods, one has to have enough room in one's stomach the way the empty space in oriental pictures give us room for spare. 'A bucket that is full to the brim has no room for holding more water and so does our yearning for everything.'

The Last Letters 5 minutes permitting

41
완벽하기만을 바라지 마라

We want to have our cake
and eat it too.

우리는 전쟁에 나가서 완벽한 승리를 바라듯이 항상 완벽하길 바랍니다. 모든 일에 대해 100퍼센트 완벽하길 바라는 것은 희망사항이지만, 51퍼센트 성공에 49퍼센트 실패의 확률도 있는 법입니다. 100퍼센트 바라는 사람은 언제든 완벽한 실패도 맛볼 수 있습니다. 욕심이 항상 문제입니다. 자제를 배워야 합니다. 맛있는 음식을 즐기려면 시장이 반찬이라지 않습니까? 공간의 여백이 동양화의 미덕이지 않습니까? '다 찬 물통은 더 이상 물을 담을 수 없고, 욕망도 마찬가지입니다. 작은 일에 만족할 줄 알아야 합니다.'

If you want him to be a fisherman,
You've got to make him love the sea.

돛배타기
Sailing

어부가 되기 위해서는
To be a fisherman

그가 어부가 되기를 원한다면,
먼저 바다를 사랑하게 해라.

파도타기
Surfing

수영
Swimming

물고기잡기
Fishing

Nobody is perfect except God and we often face defeats in many occasions. In conquest of our happiness we have to learn how to handle the failure we face in our lives. Life itself is a learning process. 'We are here in the universe to learn lessons and people and things are our teachers.' It is a wise attitude to learn from our failure rather than losing our heart. Changing our attitudes toward our failure is the first thing we have to do before we decide when we are going to try the same thing again which we failed in the first attempt. Failure shows us the way that we have to follow for success. Our frame of mind gives us the essential ingredients for success. William James told us that it is our mental attitude which determines the failure or success in all events of life. Think failure as a detour and make it as a stepping stone for our quantum jump toward days to come.

The Last Letters 5 minutes permitting

42
실패는 돌아가는 길이다

Think of failure as a detour.

어느 누구도 신 이외에는 완벽한 사람이란 없습니다. 인간이기 때문에 많은 일에 실패하는 것은 당연합니다. 중요한 건 행복하기 위해서 실패에 어떻게 대응하느냐입니다. '나는 이 세상에 배우러 왔으며, 매일매일 만나는 사람들과 일어나는 일들은 나의 소중한 선생님입니다.' 실패하면 실패로부터 배우면 됩니다. 가슴앓이를 하는 것보다 훨씬 현명한 대처지요. 실패는 성공의 길을 알려줍니다. 계속 강조하지만 문제는 실패가 아니라 우리의 마음자세입니다. 우리의 마음의 틀이 실패냐 성공이냐를 결정한다고 윌리엄 제임스는 이야기합니다. 실패는 돌아가는 길이라 생각하고, 이 실패를 디딤돌로 삼아 내일은 큰 도약을 하십시오.

If one goes mountain climbing, one has to be the mountain which one climbs. If one plays the piano, one has to be the piano which he or she plays. Our lives are falling apart when the fragmentation starts in what we do in life. Being melted together as one is the only way to live our lives to their fullest. We live in a world with a deluge of choices and we are being lost in choosing how to live a life. 'Just imagine an eagle taking its flight. It does not leave a trace on its flight.' Our lives have to be lived like that of an eagle in its flight. When we try to leave a mark in the history of the human, our lives become fragmented in fragments. Stay in tune with the rhythm of the life and enjoy the full flavor of life to its fullest.

The Last Letters 5 minutes permitting

43
삶을 100퍼센트 살아라
Live life to its fullest.

산을 오르면 나는 산이 되고, 피아노를 치면 나는 피아노가 됩니다. 그 순간에는 그것만 해야지 여러 가지 일을 벌려 복잡한 생각으로 어지러워지면 아무것도 이룰 수 없기 때문입니다. 지금 하고 있는 일에 함께 녹아버리면 삶을 100퍼센트 사는 것입니다. 선택의 홍수 속에 살고 있다고 해도 과언이 아닐 정도로 매일매일 선택을 시험받습니다. 그리고 곧잘 길을 잃기 일쑤입니다. '독수리가 날아가는 것을 보십시오. 독수리는 날아가면서 자국을 남기지 않습니다.' 여러 갈래로 젖어진 삶은 자국을 남기기 쉽습니다. 득수리가 날듯이 살아보십시오. 그저 삶의 리듬에 몸을 싣고, 그 리듬의 맛을 마음껏 즐기며, 기쁘게 날아가십시오.

The darkest moment of one's life can be the turning moment of one's life when one changes one's attitude. A beaming smile can be appreciated without seeing a frowning face. Nothing stays permanent and it is the life. Life has to go on and one has to adapt to it if one wants to stay in the road of life. There are many phases of life and each phase has its own mode of adaptation. 'One has to master the ways and means to overcome hard tasks of life. A nutshell of life is just keeping it up till the end with a positive mental frame of mind,' There is no one in the universe without any problem of life that has to be solved. One can not achieve a thing without helping hands of others. Hitting the bottom means only up is on way to go. This may be the solace to all of us. God is real and we feel the tender touch of His in a difficult time. The brightest star can be seen in the darkest sky.

The Last Letters 5 minutes permitting

44
가장 밝은 별은 가장 어두운 하늘에서 보인다

The brightest star can be seen in the darkest sky.

아무리 상황이 나쁘고 최악이라 해도 스스로 마음먹기에 따라 얼마든지 좋은 방향으로 바꿀 수 있습니다. 잠시라도 찌푸린 얼굴을 하면 밝은 얼굴이라 느낄 수 없습니다. 항상 밝게 웃으십시오. 모든 것은 항상 변합니다. 그것이 인생입니다. 인생이라는 길 위에서 존재하려면 부단히 변해야 합니다. 그것이 우의의 숙명입니다. 삶이란 기쁨과 슬픔의 여러 국면이 있고, 그 상황에 맞게 대처해야 합니다. 특히 '어려운 상황을 돌파할 수 있는, 이길 수 있는 방법을 알아야 합니다. 한마디로 말하면, 죽는 날까지 긍정적인 자세를 잃지 않으면 됩니다. 밑바닥을 치면 올라갈 일만 남았습니다.' 무엇보다 이 사실이 큰 위안이 됩니다. 더불어 아주 힘들 때야 비로소 하나님이 계시다는 것을 느낄 수 있습니다. 어떤 의미에서 힘든 순간은 크나큰 축복이라 할 수 있습니다. 가장 어두운 순간에 가장 밝은 별이 보입니다.

When our loved one dies, we find a hole in our heart and this hole can be filled by calling forth love. Love heals all wounds as time does. Without healing of our loss, our lives go astray without limit. Healing starts with our acceptance of the inevitable loss. Then fill our heart with love coming from the loved ones. A hole can be filled with something that is bigger than it. The same logic can be applied to our loss since love does have no bound and through love we can heal our wound of loss. Death can come at any moment and to anyone without notice. Thus we have to be ready to go when the death gives us a signal to go. Also we should accept the inevitable without any hassle as the sea accepts the water of the river. 'Ups and downs make waves of life and death and birth do weave a net of life.' The beginning does contain the ending like birth and death. Learn to console our loss with love and be ready to go when time ripens.

The Last Letters 5 minutes permitting

45
상실은 가슴에 구멍이 나는 것과 같다

Loss is a hole in our heart.

만약 가까이 있던 사랑하는 사람이 죽는다면 어떻겠습니까? 가슴에 커다란 구멍이 생길 것입니다. 이 구멍은 오직 사랑으로만 치유할 수 있습니다. 사랑은 시간처럼 모든 상처를 치유합니다. 상실을 치유하지 않으면 끝없이 방황하게 됩니다. 치유는 어찌할 수 없는 상실을 받아들일 수 있을 때 비로소 가능한 것입니다. 죽음은 언제 어디서나 누구에게나 올 수 있습니다. 죽음이 오라고 손짓할 때 갈 준비가 되어 있어야 합니다. 마치 바다가 강을 받아들이듯이 말입니다. '오르고 떨어지는 것, 태어나고 죽는 것, 이 모든 과정이 삶이라는 그물을 엮는 날줄과 씨줄입니다.' 죽음을 슬퍼하지 마십시오. 상실은 사랑으로 극복하고, 때가 되면 우리도 죽을 준비를 해야 합니다.

A fine paticle can be obtained through many diffenrent sizes of sieve.
The wisdom we need for life's journey has been gotten
for many generations of filtering processes.

Tao te ching, The art of war, I-Ching and Talmud
give us the wisdom filtered through fine sieves.

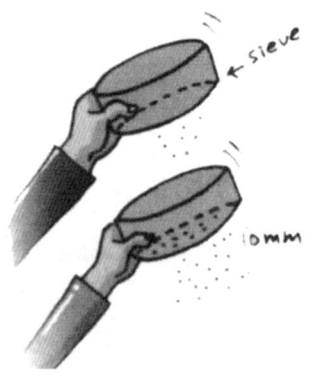

물건을 걸러내는 체
Filtering

고운 가루는 여러 번 체를 쳐야 얻을 수 있다.
삶의 여정에 필요한 지혜도 여러 세대를 거치면서 걸러진 것이다.

도덕경, 손자병법, 주역, 탈무드는 모두 고운 체에 걸러진 지혜이다.

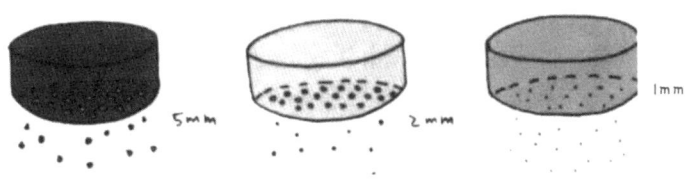

출처 : 만화 30원(야스미디어)

'We are here in this planet to learn some lessons. Lessons will be learned through many means. Two most important means of learning is to learn from people we meet and through books we read.' If we are learner, our days will be all exciting thanks to our joy felt in our heart. Life gives us endless joy if we are willing to learn new things that are available to us. The view of the window will be different if we change the color of the window glass.

Also we can see different things if we look through our window at different positions. This will give us ways to multiply our joy in life. By learning foreign language, we can learn another world and through this world our scope of vision will be enlarged for our own joy. Learn as much as we can if we have chances of learning so that every moment of our days will be the best moment of our lives. Life consists of seas of moment and learning a new thing will give us pleasure derived from the learning. Be a lifelong learner and enjoy the life.

The Last Letters 5 minutes permitting

46
영원히 살 것처럼 배워라

Learn as if you expected to live forever.

'우리가 이 지구라는 행성에 태어난 이유 중 하나는 배우기 위함입니다. 배움의 방향은 여러 가지인데, 그중 최고는 만남을 통해 배우는 것이고, 또 하나는 책을 읽고 배우는 것입니다.' 무엇을 배운다는 것은 얼마나 가슴이 벅차고 흥분되는 일입니까? 배우려 하는 마음으로 가득하면 그보다 더 큰 즐거움이 있겠습니까? 창틀 유리와 색깔을 바꾸면, 세상은 달라보입니다. 또한 보는 위치를 바꾸어도 전혀 새롭게 보이지요. 배움도 이런 논리입니다. 외국어를 배우면 새로운 세상이 열리고, 세상을 보는 눈이 확연히 달라집니다. 열심히 배우십시오. 평생 배우십시오. 배움은 세상의 가장 큰 즐거움입니다.

Sometimes decision making is harder than solving the knotty day-to-day problems. When we can hear the inner voice of ours, it is simple to make decision on all matters of life. Life is flowing according to our decisions and the right decision making is the pertinent matter in life. 'The path we took in the forked road will lead us to the sea or to the mountain because a small deviation at the beginning will make a great difference in the end. Thus we have to master the art of decision making for our days to come.' The first step toward a good decision making is to see things in an objective view rather than subjective view point. Unbiased views lead us to a good decision on all matters since our attachment toward matters will bend the right path of making wise decisions. The calm surface of the lake reflects a perfect image and so does our decision made by listening to the inner voice of ours. When we sit and do meditation, the inner voice of ours will be heard. The second step to listen to the inner voice of ours is to empty ourselves on all matters so that nothing disturbs us from inside of us.

The Last Letters 5 minutes permitting

47
내면의 소리에 귀를 기울여라

Listen to the inner voice of yours.

가끔은 결정을 한다는 것이 날마다의 힘든 문제를 해결하는 것보다 힘들 때가 있습니다. 만약 자신의 내면의 소리를 둘을 수 있다면 삶의 모든 문제의 결정을 내리는 일이 간단해집니다. 삶은 우리의 결정에 따라 흐르고 결정을 잘 내린다는 것은 삶에서 중요한 문제입니다. 갈림길에서 나의 결정에 따라 바다로도, 또는 산으로도 갈 수 있습니다. 왜냐하면 '처음의 조그마한 엇갈림이 끝에는 크나큰 차이를 만듭니다. 따라서 내일을 위해서는 결정을 잘하는 기술이 매우 필요합니다.' 중요한 것은 편견 없는 시각이 좋은 결정에 이르게 한다는 겁니다. 어디에 집착하면 그 집착이 바른 결정을 못 하게 합니다. 잔잔한 수면이 완벽한 상을 형성하듯이, 내면의 소리가 완벽한 결정을 합니다. 내면의 소리를 잘 들을 수 있는 방법은 바로 참선입니다. 스스로를 비울 때, 몸과 마음을 평온하게 하고 자연스럽게 내면의 소리도 둘을 수 있습니다.

A short person can do better going through a small door, but he or she might have some inconvenience in placing a thing high on a shelf. A tall person might have other one. When our limitations cause difficulties in life, we have to find ways to circumvent the problems. The saying goes, "Where there is a will, there is a way." The first step is to accept our limitation. Once we know our limitation, we can figure out the ways to tackle the problem. If we are willing to tackle the knotty problems in life, we always find the way to solve the problems. God gives us the strength along with the faith that we can do all things with His help. If one can not alter the situation, one has to change oneself to fit in the situation. 'There is an old Korean saying that one has to eat foods with gums if he or she does not have teeth. There is more than one way to reach the peak of the mountain and so do our limitations to solve the problems of life. Our limitations give us a chance to hone our skills tackling problems of life.'

The Last Letters 5 minutes permitting

48
주어진 한계를 즐겨라

Enjoy the limitation that is given to us.

키가 작은 사람은 작은 문도 잘 빠져나갈 수 있지만 높은 선반에 물건을 올려놓을 때는 매우 불편합니다. 키가 큰 사람 역시 똑같은 문제가 역으로 생깁니다. 즉 작은 문을 지나기는 힘들지만, 높은 곳에 물건을 올려놓는 일은 매우 쉽지요. 능력의 한계가 불편함을 주면, 돌아가는 법을 배우면 됩니다. 뜻이 있는 곳에 길이 있다는 속담이 있듯이, 우선 자신의 한계를 인정해야 합니다. 한계를 알면, 한계를 극복하는 방법을 알 수 있습니다. 문제를 극복할 의지가 있다면, 힘든 문제를 풀 수 있는 방법을 기어코 찾아내고야 맙니다. 하나님은 도움의 손길로 모든 일을 할 수 있는 힘과 믿음을 주십니다. 상황을 변화시킬 수 없다면, 상황에 따라 변해야 합니다. '한국 속담에 이런 말이 있습니다. "이가 없다면 잇몸으로 먹어야 한다." 한계가 우리의 기술을 더 숙련되게 해서 삶의 문제를 푸는 열쇠가 됩니다.'

When we are eager to hear the praise of others, we can not show the best of ourselves in doing things. It is commonly said that if you are in a baseball game, do as if you do a workout and in doing a workout you do as if you are in a baseball game. There is a saying and it goes "Too much strain broke the rope." Trying to show off our talents to others puts a stain on us. It is wise to present ourselves to others without our frills. The real characters of a horse can be found without a rider on its saddle. A scenic view of a river can be seen when we put nothing in its passage. Foods with a lot of MSG give us an artificial flavor and we become sick of it soon. 'Mother Nature gives us a direction on how to live our lives but we try and try to do our own way. Sing as if no one can hear you and lead a wonderful life.'

The Last Letters 5 minutes permitting

49
아무도 듣지 않는다고 생각하고 노래해라

Sing as if no one can hear you.

남의 칭찬에 연연하면 어떤 일을 할 때 최선을 다하지 못하게 됩니다. 야구시합을 할 때는 연습장에 있는 것처럼 하고, 연습장에서는 시합장에 있는 것처럼 하라는 말이 있지요? 줄에 너무 많은 힘을 가하면 줄이 동강난다는 속담이 있습니다. 남에게 더 잘하려고 하면 할수록 긴장하게 됩니다. 있는 모습을 그대로 보여주어야 합니다. 멋진 강의 경치는 보이는 길에 쓸데없는 물건이 없어야 잘 보입니다. 음식에 조미료를 너무 많이 치면, 음식의 진짜 맛은 없고 가짜 맛이 생기고 곧장 싫증이 납니다. '자연은 인간에게 어떻게 살라는 방향을 주지만, 어리석은 사람들은 자기 식대로 살려고 발버둥 칩니다. 그러니 노래를 잘하려면, 아무도 듣는 사람이 없다고 생각할 때 잘 부를 수 있습니다.'

You can't lose the weight of your mind by taking off your clothes.
If you want to make your mind lighter,
you get rid of worry, hate, discontentment
and vanity or you load your mind
with thankfulness, humbleness, courage, truthfulness and hope.

출처 : 만화 30원(야스미디어)

치루를 벗고
No coat

내 마음의 무게는?
The weight of my mind?

옷을 벗는다고 마음의 무게가 가벼워지지는 않는다.

마음의 주머니에서 근심, 미움, 불만, 허영 등
   마음을 무겁게 하는 것들을 덜어내고

감사, 겸손, 용기, 진실, 희망 등을 채우면
   마음의 무게는 점점 가벼워진다.

바지를 벗고
No trousers

알몸으로
Naked

Our days on earth are numbered and we have to spend each day fully satisfied. The first step is to live one day at a time. 'Living one day at a time means finishing each day and be done with it.' No more or no less efforts are needed for this job. Each moment is precious and learning the value of each moment is more important. When one lives a day fully satisfied, one gets the happiness and bliss coming from our Creator. A spent day is like a spent check and we can do nothing about it. Do enjoy every moment of yours like the last moment of yours for your own good. Learning to find the joy of each fleeting moment is easy if you open your heart fully toward everything without any prejudiced ideas. The ocean gets its water from all sources without any discrimination like a mother hugs her child. Opening our heart is the starting point of our race for love toward others. Just finish each day and be done with it. Also love every moment with all your heart to add the finishing touch on your finishing day.

The Last Letters 5 minutes permitting

50
날마다 딱 한 번의
하루를 끝내라

Finish each day and be done with it.

사는 날은 정해져 있으므로, 날이면 날마다 만족스럽게 살아야 합니다. 한 번에 하루만 사십시오. '한 번에 하루만 산다는 이야기는 날마다 하루를 끝내고 그 하루는 끝난 것으로 생각하라는 이야기입니다.' 모든 순간은 귀중하고, 그리고 그 순간의 가치를 배우는 것도 중요합니다. 하루를 완벽하게 살았다면, 창조주의 은총과 행복을 얻을 것입니다. 이미 보내 버린 하루는 사용한 수표와 같아서 어떤 일도 할 수 없습니다. 매 순간을 마치 마지막 순간인 것처럼 즐기십시오. 빨리 지나가는 순간을 가슴을 열고 아무런 편견 없이 즐길 줄 알아야 합니다. 바다는 모든 것으로부터 물을 받아들이는데 마치 엄마가 아이를 안듯이 편견 없이 받아들입니다. 다른 사람을 사랑하는 첫 시작은 가슴을 여는 것입니다. 하루를 하루로 살고, 잊어버립시다. 모든 순간을 사랑하고 그러고 가슴에 끝나는 날의 끝마무리를 해야 합니다.

During our days on earth we go over many severe pains and every pain gives us a lesson. Learning a lesson is living a life. Life's lesson is like an unfinished project and we have to go over till we die. Pain shows us how to react on specific situation and makes us get prepared for the upcoming events. When we experience pains in our lives, we start to grow and this growth makes us better person. We have a saint and a devil in us and we have to struggle to get rid of a devil in us for our own good. Pains enlarge our visions on life such that we can have a better view on life in general. Going through tough times makes us tough so that we can be a safe shelter for the needy. Pains purify our heart such that we love everyone unconditionally the way God loves us. 'We have potentials to develop and pain gives us a chance to reveal our hidden potentials. Treat pain as a teacher and be a winner in life. A full life is the one full of pain and we just accept it and act accordingly.'

The Last Letters 5 minutes permitting

51
아픔을 선생님으로 대접해라
Treat pain as a teacher.

인생은 고통이라 할 수 있습니다. 하지만 이 고통을 겪으면 많은 새로운 사실을 일깨워줍니다. 인생은 이 가르침을 배우는 일이라고 할 수 있습니다. 삶의 가르침은 우리가 죽는 날까지 가는 미완성의 일입니다. 이 가르침은 다가오는 일을 준비하게 합니다. 우리는 아픔을 통해서 성장하고 이를 통해 보다 나은 인간이 될 수 있습니다. 우리의 내면에는 악마와 성인이 함께 공존합니다. 그러나 우리는 투쟁으로 이 악마를 없애려고 노력합니다. 아픔은 시야를 넓히고 그래서 삶을 더 잘 관조할 수 있게 만듭니다. 힘든 시간이 지나면서 더욱 더 강해지고, 나아가 힘든 이의 안식처가 되어줄 수 있습니다. 아픔은 우리를 순화시켜 하나님처럼 모든 이를 무조건적으로 사랑하게 만듭니다. '아픔을 통해서 잠재된 가능성을 개발시킬 수 있습니다. 아픔을 선생으로 대하여 삶의 승자가 되십시오. 완전한 삶은 아픔이 많으니 그냥 받아들이고, 그에 따라 행동하십시오.'

In starting a new project in our lives, we often find that the first step is the hardest. There is a Korean saying that if you start a job, it is half done. When we want to go on a voyage toward the uncharted sea, we often delay the departure due to our fear of the unknown. It is the same with everything in life. The saying goes that measure twice and cut once. It is wise to think much before taking action but too much thinking will achieve nothing. Practice taking action in any project such that action achieves some results. Action always beats inaction in our lives. In boxing match the first blow is the hardest and we do learn the art of boxing through it. Once you make the first step on your rung of ladder of life, you really start your life. Do start your life and enjoy the fruit of life. Without beginning there is no ending the way our birth starts our lives. 'When we get over the hardest part of our lives, our lives will be with the wind and we will enjoy our voyage on an uncharted sea of life.'

The Last Letters 5 minutes permitting

52
첫걸음이
가장 힘든 법이다

The first step is the hardest.

시작이 반이라는 한국 속담도 있듯이, 모든 일은 처음 내딛을 때가 가장 힘든 법입니다. 미지의 바다를 항해한다면 두려움으로 출발이 늦어질 수 있습니다. 속담에 자르기 전 두 번 재라는 이야기가 있지만, 심사숙고만이 능사는 아닙니다. 너무 생각만 하여 행동에 옮기지 못하면 아무것도 이룰 수 없습니다. 그러니 행동에 옮기는 추진력을 키워 무엇이라도 이루십시오. 가만히 있는 것보다 행동으로 옮기는 것이 더 이득입니다. 권투를 배울 때 처음 날린 주먹은 매우 센 법이고 이 첫 주먹을 상기하며 권투의 모든 기술을 연마하게 되지요. '인생이라는 사다리에 첫발을 걸치는 것만으로도 삶의 열매를 맛볼 수 있는 첫발을 당당히 내딛은 것입니다.'

Life starts with birth and ends with deattu What do we have to do in our lives? Learn to enjoy the process of life. Life is composed of sea of moments and we have to learn to enjoy every moment in its fullness. During our lives we go through many things and each thing requires time to ripe. Everything in life has grown to maturity with many steps of processes along with time. All we have to do in life is just enjoying the process itself rather than the end results. Do not postpone living the life since no one knows when we have to go and we might end up with unfinished project of our lives. When we have our own sons and daughters, we have a lot of joy in the process of raising them. Our grown up children give us different kinds of joy. 'Thus we have to be ready to enjoy joy of all kinds that are coming all through our lives rather than waiting for the end. Each stage of life gives us different kinds of joy and we just learn to enjoy the process of life.'

The Last Letters 5 minutes permitting

53
삶의 전 과정을 철저히 즐겨라

Enjoy the process of life.

우리는 어머니의 뱃속에 태어나서 죽음으로 삶을 마칩니다. 그런 삶을 어떻게 살아가야 할까요? 한 방울의 물들이 모여 바다를 이루듯, 우리의 삶도 순간순간의 과정들이 모여 형성됩니다. 그러므로 순간순간을 성실하게 맞이하여 100퍼센트 즐기며 살아야 합니다. 우리가 성숙해지려면 과정을 거쳐야 하고 시간이 흘러야 합니다. 삶의 과정을 겪는 것이 결과보다 즐겁고 중요한 의미를 갖습니다. 아들딸을 키워보니 어려서는 키우는 즐거움이 크고 자라서는 또 다른 즐거움을 주더군요. '삶도 모든 과정이 각각 다른 즐거움을 줍니다. 그 즐거움을 하나라도 놓치지 말고 최선을 다해 누리십시오.'

Everyone needs love in this journey we may call life. Our lives should have the experience of love. Find love in giving rather than receiving and give love unconditionally without any holdback. Conditions on love strain our relationships. We must get rid of the conditions we put on for our love. Now we take a long look at our lives and find moments that we withheld our love because of conditions we put on. These conditions put a barrier for us to open our heart to others and we missed the chance to share our love. Love that we seek is the one based on who we are rather than what we do. When we love someone, we love him or her just the way he or she is. Expectations on others are weights on our love and they block us from opening our heart to others. Let us have the experience of loving and being loved. The more love we give, the more love we feel. The more love we feel, it becomes easier for us to love others without any conditions. 'If we love someone, we must love him or her with all our heart since someone we love is given to us temporary. Find peace and happiness in love that God gives us free.'

The Last Letters 5 minutes permitting

54
사랑에서 평화와 행복을 마음껏 누려라

Find peace and happiness in love.

사랑 없이 살아가는 삶을 상상해보십시오. 사랑 없이 살아가는 삶은 아무런 의미가 없습니다. 사랑은 주는 것이 받는 것보다 더 행복하고, 무조건적으로 사랑할 때 아름답습니다. 조건이 낀다면 관계는 힘들어집니다. 조건은 가슴을 열고 진정으로 사랑하는 데 방해가 되고 장벽이 됩니다. 상대방의 있는 모습 그대로 사랑하십시오. '조금 사랑하지 말고 100퍼센트 완전히 사랑하십시오. 그리고 하나님이 공짜로 주신 사랑으로 평화와 행복을 마음껏 누리시지요.'

도끼를 갈아서
바늘을 만드는
정성으로
넘기 귀한 나눔도
지상에 天國이
올 때까지
계속하시지요.

Freh.
2005. 준산

출처: 나눔그림(아름다운재단, 콩반쪽)

The life we create is based on our belief. The history we made is founded on belief on many.

If we have faith on ourselves, we can achieve an impossible task. The way of thinking can make us achieve a task we planned. Nothing is impossible if we believe ourselves. 'When we start a new project, we have to start with firm belief on ourselves such that a mountain can be moved thanks to our firm belief. It is wise to have faith on someone in doing something. The positive attitude will give us the faith needed in achieving a tough task.' When a task is tougher, we need stronger belief that brings a work to completion. Just imagine the final results of our project when we have a tough time in doing our projects and the visualization of our final results leads us to what we had hoped for. The belief we have on us will achieve a great work if our belief is firmly grounded on us. Do start our day with unshakeable belief on our ability.

The Last Letters 5 minutes permitting

55
자신을 믿으면
더 잘할 수 있다

We can do well
if we believe ourselves.

인류의 새로운 역사는 많은 사람들의 믿음 속에 만들어지듯이, 우리의 삶도 믿음으로 만들어가는 것입니다. 자신을 믿으면 불가능해 보이는 일도 가능하게 됩니다. '어떤 일을 시작하면 산도 움직일 수 있다는 강한 믿음으로 시작하십시오. 긍정이 반드시 기적을 일으킵니다.' 일이 성공하게 되는 결과를 머릿속에 그림으로 그리고 일에 매진하십시오. 흔들림 없는 단호한 믿음만이 큰일을 해내게 합니다.

In the middle of darkness we can not see things clearly and the same logic will apply to a critical moment of our lives. 'Instead of cursing a misfortune of our lives, we need an antidote against it. Darkness can be eliminated by lighting a candle. Thus we must learn to nullify a thing with its complementary measure.' Life shows us the existing symmetry of matters and events such that we can find ways or means to cope with our difficult matters of life. Life has to be lived and it has means to fulfill its destiny. Let us face the life with determination to cope with it rather than take flight. Try to find antidotes against the difficult matters of our lives so our lives will be brighter than before. Even in a cloudy day we firmly believe the existence of sun behind the cloud. This is the life we have to live well with a candle of hope in our hand.

The Last Letters 5 minutes permitting

56
어둠을 벗어나려면 촛불을 켜라

Light a candle if we want to eliminate darkness.

어둠 속에서는 사물을 잘 볼 수 없습니다. 마찬가지로 인생에 위기가 찾아오면 당장 앞을 구분하기도 힘들어집니다. 그러나 '어둠은 촛불을 켜면 사라지듯이, 불행을 비난하기보다는 위기를 극복하는 방법을 빨리 찾아야 합니다. 즉 모든 일을 반대급부를 이용하여 힘없게 만드는 지혜가 필요합니다.' 여러 번 되풀이 이야기하지만 우리 인생은 대칭으로 존재합니다. 힘들어도 살아가야 하고 피할 수 없는 운명이라면, 도망가지 말고 당당하게 맞서 강하게 대적하십시다. 무엇이 두려울 것이 있겠습니까? 구름 낀 날에도 구름 뒤의 해가 있다는 사실을 더욱 강하게 믿읍시다. 손에 희망의 촛불 하나씩 들고 잘살아야 하는 것이 삶입니다.

When life gives us a lemon, we have to make lemonade out of it. When we are down, we have no alternatives but to go up. 'Life gives us many things to handle and all we have to do is finding the way to handle them properly. The frame of mind is the most important thing in coping with matters of life.' When we meet a wall that blocks our way, we must find ways to go over the wall. Whenever we go over obstacles in life, life offers us a new beginning that will enrich our lives like warm spring after cold winter. Do accept things as they come and just enjoy doing things in life like a flowing boat in the river. God will lead our lives when we do our part right. Tough problems in life change with time and so do our ways of handling things. Do believe that we can handle anything in life without any difficulty. Also always see the positive side of the matters and be the tough optimist. Miracles happen if we firmly believe them.

The Last Letters 5 minutes permitting

57
사막을 만나면 정원으로 만들어라

When we meet a desert,
make it a garden.

힘든 일이 주어지면 이 힘든 일도 나에게 유익한 일로 만들 줄 아는 지혜가 필요합니다. 만약 우리가 지금 내리막길에 있다면 이제는 올라갈 일만 남아 있습니다. '삶이란 미묘하게 즐거운 일 어려운 일 모두 겪는데 일마다 잘 다룰 줄 아는 선수가 되어야 합니다. 무엇보다 마음이 중요합니다.' 장벽을 만나면 장벽을 지나가는 길을 찾으면 됩니다. 추운 겨울이 지나면 따뜻한 봄이 온다는 사실도 잊지 마십시오. 강한 긍정과 믿음은 기적을 만들어냅니다. 인생을 살다 보면 별별 일들이 많지요? 하지만 이 별별 일들 모두 마치 강이 배를 품고 흐르듯이 자연스럽게 받아들입시다. 하나님은 우리가 맡은 소임에 최선을 다하면 반드시 좋은 곳으로 인도하십니다.

When you scold someone,
the threefold of bad things will return to you.

When you hit someone,
the fourfold of violence will return to you.

The more fingers point back at you
when you do more harm to others.

더 많은 숫자의 손가락이 당신을 향한다.
The more fingers point back at you

타인을 비방하기 위한 손가락질,
그 비방은 3배로 당신에게 되돌아온다.

타인을 때리기 위해 쥔 주먹,
그 폭력은 4배의 폭력으로 당신에게 되돌아온다.

당신이 더 많은 나쁜 일을 하면,
더 많은 손가락이 당신을 향한다.

출처: 만화 30원(야스미디어)

죽기 전에 해야 할 77가지

'When one wants to succeed in one's life, one has to find a new field which has never been trodden by anyone.' In a nutshell, one has to go over many fields which have been trodden by many. It is not easy to find a new path for one's life but it is possible if one struggles hard to find one. The road less traveled can be revealed to the one who is willing to go an extra mile for it. Life shows us the way where one has to go when one tries hard to find it. There is no royal road to success but the timeless principles of success have existed. The first step is to go over all the existing roads to success along with going over the life of many successful individuals. This shows us the uncharted lands to be discovered. Also we have to read many books so that we can find a new field to build our lives in. The more we are informed, the easier we can find the way to success. Every great thing starts with a thought and this thought can be found in the unlimited struggles of yours. This thought is powered into realization by the unfailing belief in yourself. Go where no one could go and make your life more enjoyable in the days to come.

The Last Letters 5 minutes permitting

58
남이 갈 수 없는 곳으로 가야 성공할 수 있다

To go where other people could not go.

'성공하려면 남이 가지 않은 길을 개척해야 합니다.' 남이 가지 않은 길을 발견한다는 것은 쉬운 일이 아닙니다. 그러나 열심히 노력하면 가능합니다. 가지 않은 길은 남보다 좀 더 노력하는 이에게 보입니다. 첩경이란 없습니다. 하지만 비결은 있지요. 첫 번째 비결은 지금껏 검증된 성공한 사람들의 길을 답습해보는 방법입니다. 남이 가지 않은 길이 보이게 됩니다. 두 번째 비결은 다독을 통해 찾는 방법입니다. 세 번째 비결은 많은 정보를 취합하여 발견하는 방법입니다. 마지막으로 명상을 통해 보이게 됩니다. 명상으로 얻은 생각이 믿음으로 힘을 받으면 현실로 나타납니다. 남이 가지 않은 길로 가서 미래에 행복한 삶을 누리시지요.

Life sets us a challenge to test our courage and willingness to grow. When a challenge is given to us in our lives, we just accept it as our lot. It is waste of time just waiting for the right time to tackle the challenge given to us. The first step is having the right set of mind. Then figure out how to handle the challenge. God never gives us a challenge which is beyond our reach. We can do everything if we think we can and nothing prevents us conquering the challenge we face. Almighty gives us all the resources for us to use in handling the knotty challenges in life. 'Be willing to invest to grow such that the more challenging problems will be yours to handle in the days to come. Never ever give up in dealing with the toughest challenge in your life. Just remember nothing can defeat you but your feeble mind.'

The Last Letters 5 minutes permitting

59
새로운 도전을
감사하게 받아라

The challenge will not wait.

인생이라는 무대에서 우리가 더 커나가고 강해지기 위해서는 도전이라는 시험이 반드시 필요합니다. 도전이 오면 운명으로 즐겁게 받아들여야 합니다. 나중에 도전할 더 좋은 시간이 있다고 미루는 것은 시간낭비입니다. 도전이 오면 마음의 준비를 단단히 하고 어떻게 대응할지 찬찬히 연구해야 합니다. 하나님은 해결 못 할 도전을 우리에게 주시지 않습니다. 어떤 도전도 감당할 수 있을 정도입니다. 우리에게는 감당해낼 충분한 자질을 하나님께 이미 받았습니다. '도전을 즐기시지요. 힘든 문제와 부닥치면 절대 포기하지 마십시오. 연약한 마음만 아니면 반드시 극복됩니다.'

Our desire for rich knows no bound and we are struggling all through our lives to amass a fortune. The first step is to empty ourselves as empty as possible so that we may have space to pile our fortune up. A new idea will be popped up when our brain has room to store. An empty bottle has more room to fill and the more room we have the more good things we can store. 'Life gives us unlimited resources of pleasure along with happiness when we have room for accommodation. Let us try as empty as possible so God fills us up with His blessings.'

The Last Letters 5 minutes permitting

60
가능한 한 많이 비워두어라
Let us remain as empty as possible.

부자가 되고 싶은 욕망은 끝이 없고 사람들은 일생을 이 욕망을 채우기 위해 투쟁합니다. 될 수 있는 한 많이 비워서 재물을 쌓을 공간이 없도록 비워둡시다. 우리의 뇌가 텅 비면 새로운 생각이 샘솟듯 떠오르게 되지요. 텅 빈 병은 많은 것을 저장할 수 있습니다. '포용할 줄 아는 관용이 있다면 더 많은 즐거움과 행복이 기다립니다. 가능한 한 많이 비워두어 하나님이 주시는 축복으로 가득 채우십시오.'

'God is our creator and He has made us a perfect creature such that we can be the winner in journey called life.' **Make sure that** you have all the ingredients for success in business termed as life. Each one of us was given the unique talent for living the life on earth and all we have to do is finding the God given talents. This finding of our talents might take all of our lives but we have to find them for our own good. We have to pass many roads to find the hidden treasure of ours. Do not get hurry in finding this treasure because you might lose yourself on the way.

The Last Letters 5 minutes permitting

61
우리는 무한한 가능성을 가진 한 사람의 신이다

You are one of the Lords of the earth
with unlimited potentials.

'하나님은 우리가 인생이라는 무대에서 성공하도록 완벽하게 만드셨습니다.' 인생이란 업종에서 성공할 수 있는 모든 자질을 주셨습니다. 모두가 자신만의 독특한 재능을 가지고 태어났습니다. 이 재능을 발견하는 데 일생을 보낼 수도 있겠지만, 자신을 위해서 빨리 찾아야 합니다. 숨겨진 보석 같은 재능을 찾기 위해 시행착오의 수순을 밟아봐야 합니다. 하지만 너무 급하게 서두르면 가는 중에 길을 잃어버릴 수도 있으니 조심하십시오.

When we face problems that have to be solved, we have to have facts on problems to solve. Many will dream of rosy facts of the problems and do not get the desired results. We have to remember that facts are far more important than our wishful dreams. In dealing with matters in life in general we have to have factual things first and then start to attack the problems in hand. A map is needed in order to climb a mountain but the map does not give us the detailed information on terrain of the mountain. 'Learn to go over the firsthand experiences of a thing rather than the secondhand one since seeing is one thing and hearing is another on all matters in life. Try to go over more direct experiences than vicarious ones for your ability for solving problems of life.'

The Last Letters 5 minutes permitting

62
사실들이 꿈보다 더 중요하다
Facts are better than dreams.

문제를 풀려면 그 문제에 관련된 사실들을 알아야 합니다. 많은 사람들이 문제의 허상만을 알고 있어서 문제를 잘 풀지 못합니다. 사실이 우리가 원하는 허상과는 많이 다르다는 사실을 알아야 합니다. 실생활의 문제는 사실에 기준한 일들로 풀어야 합니다. 산을 올라가려면 지도가 필요합니다만, 지도는 산의 지형을 완벽하게 정확히 알려주지 못합니다. 그러니 '직접적인 경험으로 문제에 접근해야지 남을 통한 간접경험은 마치 보는 것과 듣는 것이 다른 것과 같습니다. 그러니 삶의 문제를 풀 때 직접적인 경험으로 풀도록 하십시오.'

We start the first step toward our destiny when we set our purpose in life. 'The purpose will lead us the way toward fulfilling our purpose and this is what we may call destiny.' The destiny is the fruit of our purpose in life. The purpose of our lives will generate things we need to achieve our purpose in our lives and all we have to do is follow the steps which are given to us in our days with full enthusiasm in our heart. Let us spend some of our precious time to figure out the purpose of our lives and this will shape our destiny in the days to come. There is not a thing called free lunch in life and we have to do more thinking to get the purpose of our lives. It can be reached through much reading along with much thinking and paving many roads. Do find our purpose in life and shape our destiny.

The Last Letters 5 minutes permitting

63
분명한 목표가 있기에 운명은 만들어간다

Purpose shapes destiny.

삶의 목표가 정해져야, 그 목표에 따라 비로소 삶의 첫발자국을 내밀 수 있습니다. '목표가 이끄는 방향으로 삶이 흘러가는데, 이를 두고 보통 운명이라 합니다.' 운명은 삶의 목표의 결과물입니다. 세상에는 공짜가 없습니다. 삶의 목표를 무엇으로 정해야 할지 심사숙고해야 합니다. 이를 위해서는 풍부한 독서도 필요하고, 긴 시간의 생각도 필요하고, 여러 갈래의 길을 답습해보면서 자연스레 깨우쳐집니다. 삶의 목표가 우리의 운명도 정하고 바꾸도록 만들어갑니다.

Our days are numbered and we have no days to waste in our lives. Time and monies spent on self-improvement are always wise investment. Instead of complaining on things we face in life, we have to find ways turning lemon into lemonade. The miracle happens due to the efforts of people who made it happen. The cumulative effect of daily work is the most important ingredient for the rewarding success. The road less traveled can be found through tenacious efforts of the seeker. New ideas generate opportunities for success and we can get these new ideas through many routes in other words books, people, and thinking. Do remember that every second is counted all through our lives. The big return is made through investment on improving ourselves.

The Last Letters 5 minutes permitting

64
단 일 초의 시간도 낭비하지 말고 늘 깨어서 투자해라

Do not waste and be willing to invest.

우리에게는 살아 갈 날이 이미 정해져 있어서 단 하루도 낭비할 수 없습니다. 자신을 위해 투자하는 시간과 돈은 항시 멋진 투자입니다. 우리는 어려운 문제에 부닥치면 우리가 덕을 보는 방향으로 변화시키는 방법을 알아내야 합니다. 기적은 기적을 만들어 내는 사람이 만듭니다. 날마다 쌓이는 일의 결과는 우리에게 대가를 나누어 주는 성공에 꼭 필요한 일입니다. 남이 자주 가지 않는 길은 끝없는 노력에 의해서 발견될 수 있습니다. 새로운 발상은 성공을 위한 새로운 기회를 제공하는데, 이는 책과 사람과 생각으로 얻어지는 것입니다. 단 일 초의 시간도 결코 낭비하지 마십시오. 큰 수확을 얻기 위해 늘 깨어서 자신에게 투자하는 노력을 하십시오.

The opportunities for success are given to the prepared one and luck is only a beginning for a lucky one. 'The late bloomer is the one who had spent a great amount of time and efforts on becoming winner in oner's chosen field. Just remember that luck is where preparation meets opportunity and we have to be prepared to grab the incoming opportunity.' It takes time to build a big dream and we have to have perseverance along with endurance to fulfill our dream. Ocean starts with a drop of water and so does a mountain with a handful of earth. The higher you want to go, the harder you have to struggle in your life. You need a big hook along with a big boat to catch a big fish but you have to do more to fulfill your lifers dream. Let us get more facts on your goal and act accordingly. Life is too short to wait for the right moment.

The Last Letters 5 minutes permitting

65
행운이란 시작에 불과하다
Luck is only a beginning.

성공은 준비된 자에게 오고, 행운이란 행운아에게는 단지 시작에 불과합니다. '대기만성하는 사람은 주어진 분야에서 많은 시간과 노력을 부단히 해온 사람입니다. 그러므로 이들에게 찾아오는 행운이란 기회와 준비가 절묘하게 만난 지점이라 할 수 있습니다.'

그러므로 성공하기 위해서는 평소에 기회를 잡을 준비가 완벽하게 되어 있어야 합니다. 또한 큰 꿈을 이루려면 시간이 걸리고 쉽게 포기하지 않는 인내력도 요구됩니다. 대양도 한 방울의 물로 이루어지고, 태산도 한 줌의 흙으로 만들어집니다. 성공을 위해 평소 부단히 자료를 모으고 준비하십시오. 좋은 시간이 따로 있다고 기다리기에는 우리네 인생이 결코 길지 않습니다.

The giving has to be generous and we have to practice to be generous givers. The more things we give someone in need, the more return we can expect in the coming days. Giving and receiving is a two-way street and a giving hand spins off more return. Everything in life has a symmetric nature and everything will follow the inherent nature of the symmetry. A generous giving will generate a generous return in the days to come. Let us do more giving as a savings account for our rainy days. When we are at the peak of the mountain, we have only one alternative in other words descending the mountain. Nobody knows what the next moment would generate our lot. Participating in giving when we can. 'The winners in life do prepare everything in advance and keep their winning spree. Give much and get much.'

The Last Letters 5 minutes permitting

66
평소 적게 베풀면 어려울 때 똑같은 대접을 받는다

If you give little, you will get little.

나눔은 너그럽게 해야 하므로 평소 너그럽게 주는 연습을 해야 합니다. 도움이 필요한 사람에게 더 많이 주면, 나중에 더 많은 것을 받을 수 있습니다. 세상의 모든 것은 대칭성을 가지고 있기에, 세상에 일어나는 모든 일들 또한 이 대칭의 논리를 따릅니다. 그러므로 풍요로운 나눔은 풍요로운 받음을 만드는 것이죠. 언젠가 나도 어려워질 수 있기에 평소 많이 나누어야 합니다. 내가 만약 산의 정상에 있다면, 내려가는 일만 남아 있습니다. 우리는 한 치 앞도 내다볼 수 없습니다. '승자로 남기 위해서 미리 준비해야 합니다. 많이 나누어주고, 나중에 많이 받아야 합니다.'

We often see results of something and judge it accordingly. The results we observed are not showing us how the results were obtained and often mislead us in the wrong direction. It is like judging a book by its thickness and we never know the value of a book without reading it. In making friends, we often make many mistakes due to our inability to see through a person's real value or characters. In other to judge someone, we have to have many occasions to share and many hours to get together along with a lot of traveling together. Also 'in judging someone we have to use the same standards without adulterating standards like we use a ruler for measuring a stick or a steel rod.'

The Last Letters 5 minutes permitting

67
겉으로 드러나는 현상만 보고 판단하지 말아라

Do not judge anything by appearance.

우리는 일의 결과만 보고 그 결과에 따라서만 판단을 합니다. 결과는 그 결과가 어떻게 얻어졌는지 과정을 알려주지 않습니다. 그래서 가끔 잘못 이해하게 됩니다. 마치 한 권의 책을 평가할 때 읽어보지도 않고 책의 두께로만 판단하는 것과 같습니다. 친구를 만들 때도 마찬가지입니다. 많은 시간을 함께 보내고 여행도 같이 떠나봐야 그 친구에 대해 잘 알게 됩니다. 그리고 '늘 같은 잣대로 판단해야 합니다. 마치 나무나 철을 재는 자도 같아야 되듯이 말입니다.'

If you want to b a winner in life, you have to master skills to be a master of your undertaking. 'It takes time to build something special and do not overlook the accumulative effects of daily effort of yours.' Gibbon spent twenty years to write a book titled Decline and fall of the Roman Empire. It took thirty years to finish Webster's Dictionary. As we can see many years of efforts and pain make a special thing in the history of human beings. Remember that the results of uncommon dedication to a task reward us a great triumph that is the results of our unending persistence toward a task. Just think that Rome was not built in a day and we have to do our part without interrupting our endeavors in becoming the master in our chosen field.

The Last Letters 5 minutes permitting

68
일인자가 되려면 많은 시간과 노력을 쏟아라

Be the master in whatever you undertake.

어느 분야에서든 일인자가 되기 위해서는 날마다 연마해야 하는 시간이 필요합니다. '이 연습의 시간들이 쌓이고 쌓여야만 일인자라는 목표에 다가갈 수 있음을 잊지 마십시오.' 기봉은 로마 흥망사를 쓰기 위해서 20년을 소요했고, 웹스터는 사전을 만드는 데 30년을 소요했습니다. 수많은 시간과 끊임없는 노력과 헌신만이 인류역사에서 큰 업적을 남기는 법입니다.

Love is the sharpest sword that can cut evil.

행복이란?
An eye for an eye

악을 자를 수 있는 가장 날카로운 칼은 사랑이다.

출처: 만화 30원 (야스미디어)

A new thing can be found on a road that has been less travelled and an innovative idea will be born in a brain with less worldly things. If you think like the crowd, you will lead your life just like the crowd. 'A joy-filled life will be given to you if you think differently. You are what you think and your thinking will shape your life.' If you want to think differently, you have to read a lot of books and think much. Reading and thinking will find a new road that has never been trodden. Many ways are existed to think not like the crowd and finding new ways are ours to achieve during our days on earth. A critical thinking is needed to start a new thinking and this lead us to a new idea. A role changing in a given situation can give us a new solution for knotty problems of life.

Do learn to differentiate between a solution and an easy way out of a problem such that we can have a clear view on everything we face during our lives. Sometimes emptying ourselves of everything can be a new start and do practice this more often for a new thinking.

The Last Letters 5 minutes permitting

69
남들과 똑같이 생각해서는 새로운 창조란 없다

Do not think like the crowd.

고독하지만 남이 하지 못한 생각, 남이 가지 않은 길, 세상과 거리를 둠으로써 새로운 창조가 가능합니다. '기쁨이 넘친 인생을 살고 싶습니까? 생각이 남과 다르면 됩니다. 나라는 사람은 나의 생각으로 만들어진 모습입니다.' 다르게 생각하려면 책을 많이 읽으십시오. 많이 읽고 생각하면 거짓말처럼 남이 가지 않은 새로운 길이 보입니다. 또한 가끔은 자신을 비우는 것도 새로운 길을 찾는 시작일 수 있습니다.

What would you say if a rich man leads his life simple and he distributes his wealth to the poor? His chosen poverty gives you a model to follow for better and rewarding life. You do not need much to make a living. The simpler you lead your life, the happier you may become. This simple axiom has to be remembered all through your life. Imagine if you have two mouths to feed, you need more food and drinks to supply and you have got to work longer hours to meet your daily needs. 'The simple life gives you more time to spend and think beatitude of life.' A pure heart can be made through a simple way of living. A quite moment has a cleansing power of your soul and this moment can be found in simple life. Live your life as simple as possible such that your mind is at peace.

The Last Letters 5 minutes permitting

70
자유의지대로 가난해져라

Choose poverty with poverty own free will.

진정한 부자는 담박한 삶을 즐기고, 남은 돈을 주위에 필요한 사람들에게 나누어줄 줄 압니다. 삶을 영위하는 데는 많은 것이 필요치 않고, 단순하게 욕심 없이 살수록 더욱 행복해집니다. 왜 그럴까요? 만약 우리의 입이 두 개라면 더 많은 음식물과 물이 필요하고 입의 욕구를 채우기 위해 시간이 더 소요되지요. 그러므로 '단순한 삶을 산다는 건 중요한 시간과 축복을 더 많이 가질 수 있음을 의미합니다.' 순수한 마음 역시 단순한 삶에서 생깁니다. 조용한 명상의 시간도 단순한 삶에서 가능합니다. 명상은 우리의 영혼을 맑게 해주고, 마음의 평화를 가져다줍니다.

Everything is possible if you have a will to go through hardships in achieving a task you had in mind. You can do almost anything if you have a meaning in doing a given task. You can be born again if you want to such that you lead a new life. Everything is possible if you develop the skill of action on all things you do. The brain works in terms of mental image and you do make the image you want to be and act like the image you have. If you want to be a champion, you have got to act like a champion and talk like a champion. The feeling creates the action so does the action creates the feeling. Life has a way of shaping itself to your expectations, good or bad. 'Do have a vision of your coming days and start to remake yourself for your good. The great law of creation will do you a miracle in reshaping your future.'

The Last Letters 5 minutes permitting

71
절실히 원하는 대로 말하고 행동해라

Yon can remake yourself
if you want to.

지금 하는 일이 아무리 힘들고 괴로워도 결국 참아낼 수 있는지요? 지금 하는 일이 아무리 하찮은 일이라도 나에게 의미가 있는 일인가요? 이 두 가지 질문에 모두 '예.'라고 답할 수 있다면 이 세상에 불가능한 일이란 없습니다. 방법만 안다면 원하는 일을 모두 이룰 수 있습니다. 방법은 무엇인가요? 간단합니다. 되고자 하는 모습을 머리에 주입시키고, 그려진 상태로 말하고 행동하십시오. 챔피언이 되길 원한다면 챔피언처럼 말하고 행동하면 됩니다. '절실히 바라면 행동으로 나오고, 그 행동이 그 원하는 바를 더욱 절실하게 만들어서, 마침내 성공에 다다르게 할 수 있습니다.'

Many problems in life need the decision to be made and we may spend many hours of agonizing moment for this decision. The first step of decision making is to see things in the objective way so that we are not involved deeply in the matter being decided. The second step is getting facts related to the matter not the wishful thinking of ours. 'The final step is following the voice of our heart in the decision making. Our instinct for survival knows what is best for us.' More often than not our decision does not seem right in the beginning, but in the long run it will turn out right in the end. If our decisions are right all the time, we may become the almighty God and it may be our illusion. Learn to follow the decision of our instinct through meditation practice. Meditation practice bestows us a way of emptying ourselves and allows us to see things clearly without any biased views.

The Last Letters 5 minutes permitting

72
갈림길에서 헤맬 때는 가슴이 원하는 길로 가라

When you come to a fork the road,
follow the voice of your heart.

선택의 갈림길에 설 때는 명확한 판단을 내리기가 무척 힘든 법입니다. 결정을 내리기 위해 첫 번째 생각해야 할 일은 객관적으로 문제를 파악하는 일입니다. 두 번째 할 일은 문제와 관련된 객관적 사실을 모으는 일입니다. 이때 주의할 점은 내가 원하는 사실 위주로 모아서는 안 된다는 겁니다. '마지막 할 일은 내면에서 나오는 본능의 소리에 귀를 기울이는 일입니다. 본능은 무엇이 가장 절실한지를 잘 압니다.' 이렇게 해서 내린 결정이 처음에는 잘못된 것처럼 보일 수도 있지만, 시간이 많이 흐르면 신기하게도 결국 그 결정이 옳았음을 알게 됩니다. 그런데 본능의 소리를 듣는 것이 쉽겠습니까? 본능의 소리는 참선을 통해서 배우면 됩니다. 참선은 비워서 모든 것을 편견 없이 보게 합니다.

'It is the action that comes first when you plan something for your days to come.' The action is yours to take and it is your choice. The action is needed to fulfill your dream and the timely action is the first priority in a successful career. As they said in saying, "It is easier said than done."

This tells you how hard it is to act than to say. It is the hardest for you to take the first action that is needed to start your future dream. Do think hard and do act quickly in achieving your goals in life. Time never waits for you to do something and you are the one who has to act.

The Last Letters 5 minutes permitting

73
행동은 내가 선택한 것이다
Your action is your choice.

'내 미래는 내가 하는 행동으로 이루어지는 것입니다.' 행동은 꿈을 이루기 위해 필요한 전부라고 해도 과언이 아닙니다. 속담에 말하기는 쉬워도 행동은 힘들다는 이야기도 있습니다. 이 말은 우리의 말과 생각을 정작 행동으로 옮기는 것이 힘들다는 뜻입니다. 무엇보다 처음 취하는 행동이 어렵습니다. 사려 깊게 생각하는 것도 중요하지만, 빨리 행동으로 옮기십시오. 시간은 우리를 기다려주지 않습니다.

Spare some time to listen to your loved one's problems in life. When we have problems too hard to solve, we need someone to share our problems. No problem is too big or too hard for us to solve. The problem is we need someone to listen to our stories of our lives. When we talked to someone about our knotty problems in life, the problems show us the solution by itself. Listening is an act of love and this act shows that we care about the one who is talking to us.

The Last Letters 5 minutes permitting

74
경청을 한다는 것은 사랑의 표현이다

Listening is an act of love.

시간을 내서 사랑하는 사람의 인생고민을 들어주십시오. 우리에게 너무나 풀기에 힘든 문제가 있다면, 함께 풀 사람이 절실하게 필요합니다. 어떠한 문제도 풀어내기에 너무 크거나, 너무 힘든 문제는 없습니다. 문제는 우리의 문제를 경정해줄 사람이 필요하다는 겁니다. 문제를 이야기하면서 이야기하는 중에 문제 자체가 우리에게 해법을 알려주게 됩니다. 경청은 사랑의 표현이고, 자신의 문제를 이야기하는 사람을 배려한다는 표시입니다.

The quick solution or the quick chance of success is very rare in life and we have to learn the power of waiting for the right moment of our projects in life. The preparation for the right approach toward a specific problem may take a long time and we do need the power of waiting.

If you spent your whole life toward achieving your goals in life, it is a worthwhile to do the thing you want to achieve. Life has a meaning if it has the meaning to exist. In old age many people do relax too much so that their meaning of existence may be blurred like the one who is facing the last moment of one's life. Let us do check our meaning of existence more often so that we can face the real meaning of our existence of our lives. When we find why we have to live, we can bear almost any difficulties of our lives.

The Last Letters 5 minutes permitting

75
어떠한 일도 그 일에 맞는 적절한 시간을 기다려라

We need the power of waiting
for the right moment.

인생에서 쉽사리 성공한다는 일은 드문 일입니다. 계획이 생기면 이 계획에 꼭 맞는 시간을 기다리는 힘이 필요합니다. 왜냐하면 아주 구체적인 문제는 그 문제에 맞는 시간을 찾는 데 시간이 걸리기 때문입니다. 그래서 기다림의 힘이 필요한 이유입니다. 세상에서 당신의 모든 것을 바쳐서라도 꼭 이루고자 하는 일을 성취해낼 때 말할 수 없는 보람을 느끼게 되지요. 바로 삶은 존재의 이유가 있을 때 의미를 가지게 됩니다. 사람이 늙으면 왜 사는지 마치 죽음을 앞둔 사람처럼 불분명해집니다. 그러니 우리는 존재의 의미를 자주 생각해서 우리가 왜 살아야 하는가를 한 번 더 생각해야 합니다. 우리가 왜 살아야 하는가를 알면, 우리는 어떠한 난관도 극복할 수 있습니다.

In a race we do not slow down when we approach the finishing line. The same token can be applied to our old age. Some people say that they will slow down their ways of life in their old age, because they had struggled enough in their lives. Life has to be lived and there is no stopping in living a life like a flowing river. All we can do is doing our best at every moment of our lives. Since we do not know when the final moment will come and what we do is living our lives to the full with all our might. We might make the swan song of our lives in our old age when nobody least expects it. There are many men and women who did show us the miracles of their old age in the history of human beings. Do live a life with all your might and with all your strength to the end of your life.

The Last Letters 5 minutes permitting

76
결승점에 가까이 왔다 해도 천천히 달리면 안 된다

You do not need to slow down
when you see the finishing line in a race.

달리기 선수는 경주에서 결승점에 가까이 왔다고 천천히 달리지 않습니다. 똑같은 논리가 인생에도 적용됩니다. 어떤 사람은 자신은 이미 늙었다고 이제는 천천히 느긋하게 살겠다고 합니다. 이유는 일평생을 열심히 살아왔기에 이제 됐다고 합니다. 하지만 삶은 살아야 하고 흐르는 강처럼 쉼 없이 흘러야 합니다. 그래서 우리는 항상 순간을 100퍼센트 살아야 합니다. 왜냐하면 언제 마지막 순간이 올지 모르기에 그렇습니다. 우리는 노년에 가서야 걸작을 남길 수도 있습니다. 이때는 아무도 기대하지 않기에 더 큰 일로 남게 됩니다. 많은 사람들이 늙은 나이에 기적을 남긴 이가 제법 많습니다. 그러니 최후의 순간까지 최선을 다해서 살아야 합니다.

In living your life, do not fight with your destiny. It is better to swim with the current and become one with river. The same token is applied to your lot in life. Life has to be lived and your lot or your destiny is the plan given to us by our Lord. Do believe your lot and struggle to achieve your dream just doing what befalls you in your life. It is like to swim with the current and become one with river.

The Last Letters 5 minutes permitting

77
흐르는 물결을 따라서 흐르는 강과 하나가 되어라

Swim with the current and become one with river.

삶을 살아가는 일에서 당신의 운명과 싸우지 마십시오. 강물이 흐르는 방향으로 흘러서 강과 하나가 되십시오. 똑같은 논리가 삶에도 적용됩니다. 삶은 살아야 하고 운명은 하나님이 우리에게 주신 일입니다. 당신의 운명을 믿고 당신에게 주어진 꿈을 노력해서 이루십시오. 이것은 마치 강물을 따라 흐르는 것과 같아서 강물과 하나가 되는 일입니다.

The Last Letters 5 minutes permitting

77 things to think over in life

The Last Letters 5 minutes permitting

77 things to think over in life

The Last Letters 5 minutes permitting

77 things to think over in life

The Last Letters 5 minutes permitting

77 things to think over in life

The Last Letters 5 minutes permitting

77 things to think over in life